Accountability
in Education

edited by

Leon M. Lessinger
Georgia State University

and

Ralph W. Tyler
Director Emeritus,
Center for Advanced Study in the Behavioral Sciences

Charles A. Jones Publishing Company
Worthington, Ohio

Contemporary Educational Issues
National Society for the Study of Education

Farewell to Schools??? Daniel U. Levine and
Robert J. Havighurst, Editors

Models for Integrated Education, Daniel U.
Levine, Editor

Accountability in Education, Leon M. Lessinger
and Ralph W. Tyler, Editors

PYGMALION Reconsidered, Janet D. Elashoff and
Richard E. Snow

Reactions to Silberman's CRISIS IN THE CLASSROOM,
A. Harry Passow, Editor

2 3 4 5 6 7 8 9 10 / 76 75 74 73

Library of Congress Catalog Card Number: 71-184315
International Standard Book Number: 0-8396-0014-3

Printed in the United States of America

Series Foreword

Accountability in Education is one of a group of five publications which constitute the first of a series published under the auspices of the National Society for the Study of Education. Other titles are:

Farewell to Schools??? edited by Daniel U. Levine and Robert J. Havighurst

Reactions to Silberman's CRISIS IN THE CLASSROOM, edited by Harry Passow

PYGMALION Reconsidered, by Janet D. Elashoff and Richard E. Snow

Models for Integrated Education, edited by Daniel U. Levine

For more than seventy years the National Society has published a distinguished series of Yearbooks. Under an expanded publication program, beginning with the items referred to above, the Society plans to provide additional services to its members and to the profession generally. The plan is to publish each year a series of volumes in paperback form dealing with current issues of concern to educators. The volumes will undertake to present not only systematic analyses of the issues in question but also varying viewpoints with regard to them. In this manner the National Society expects regularly to supplement its program of Yearbook publication with timely material relating to crucial issues in education.

In this volume the editors have included original papers as well as significant pieces that have previously appeared elsewhere. Various viewpoints are considered, and an effort is made to anticipate the consequences of the accountability movement.

The National Society for the Study of Education wishes to acknowledge its appreciation to all who have had a part in the preparation of this book.

Kenneth J. Rehage
for the Committee on the Expanded Publication
Program of the National Society for the Study of
Education

Contributors

Dennis D. Gooler, assistant professor of education, Instructional Technology, director, Curriculum Development Institute Syracuse University

Leon M. Lessinger, Callaway Professor of Education and Professor of Urban Life, Georgia State University

William G. Milliken, governor, state of Michigan

Ewald B. Nyquist, New York commissioner of education, president, The University of the State of New York

Russell W. Peterson, governor, state of Delaware

John W. Porter, superintendent of public instruction, state of Michigan

Albert Shanker, president, United Federation of Teachers, New York City

Ralph W. Tyler, director emeritus, Center for Advanced Study in the Behavioral Sciences

Preface

Accountability has become a major subject of educational discussion. This book undertakes to clarify the issues involved, presents some of the current proposals, and reports some of the discussions on the subject in order to furnish a useful background for further study and action.

Accountability in Education discusses the subject as seen in the 1970's and in historical perspective. Federal and state interest in accountability are explored along with recommendations, caveats, and social consequences of the accountability movement. A selected bibliography provides further guidelines for study of the practical issues and problems in accountability.

Contents

Chapter

Accountability in Education

I

Accountability
in Perspective

Ralph W. Tyler

Accountability has become a major subject of educational discussion and a focus of sharp controversies. Ten years ago, the word rarely appeared in educational publications and was not mentioned on the programs of educational organizations. The sudden emergence of the term as applied to the process and outcomes of education rather than to the use of public funds deserves an explanation.

Three recent developments appear to have influenced the current emphasis and concern with accountability: namely, the increasing proportion of the average family's income that is spent on taxes, the recognition that a considerable fraction of youth are failing to meet the standards of literacy now demanded for employment in civilian or military jobs, and the development of management procedures by industry and defense that have increased the effectiveness and efficiency of certain production organizations. These developments have occurred almost simultaneously, and each has focused public attention on the schools.

Modern urban living involves a multiplicity of public services not required or demanded in an earlier era. A generation ago, the local property tax was largely used to support schools. The other local public services were not massive or very expensive. Today the cost of all services has skyrocketed, and the public is distressed by the growing proportion of personal income that is being absorbed by taxes. Frequently, questions are raised about ways of reducing costs. Schools are asked to justify increased budgets by showing greater educational effectiveness. They are told that they must be held accountable for greater results if greater funds are to be raised. This is a new emphasis in budget discussions.

Rapid social change has also brought a different public view about the necessity of education for all children. In 1900, the majority of the U. S. labor force was unskilled; today the figure is less than 5 percent. A youth who has not attained the level of literacy characteristic of the average fifth grade child has little chance for employment. Throughout the nation, the importance of education as essential for getting and holding a job is being broadcast. At the same time, figures are published showing a disturbingly high number of youth failing to meet the educational requirements for induction into the armed services. Manpower training programs for the unemployed have in many cases found that their enrollees lacked basic literacy and were unable to proceed with the training courses until they learned to read and compute. Parents from minority groups are aroused by the recognition that many of their children are not making progress in school, and many are not reading or showing other expected educational attainments.

Parents of the disadvantaged are demanding that the schools educate their children. In several cities, they have protested to the Board of Education that the schools do not report to the public the numbers of pupils who are not succeeding. They are pressing for independent audits of what is being learned by those from minority groups. They are pressing schools to take responsibility for educating their children and to be accountable for the results of their efforts. This is another new demand made on the schools.

The development of management procedures in industry and defense have emphasized strategic planning in which the over-all goals of the organization are made clear and the goals for each unit are spelled out. Then, the plans for meeting the goals are designed and as each year proceeds, periodic appraisals of the attainment or progress toward the goals are made. Each unit of the organization as well as the total organization is accountable for reaching the goals that have been established and, if a periodic measurement shows failures in attainment, attention and effort are focused on these units to explain the discrepancies and to devise practicable plans for overcoming them. In essence, these procedures that have worked well in certain areas emphasize: clarifying goals, designing plans for attaining them, measuring progress toward them, diagnosing difficulties, and redesigning the plan, with subsequent appraisal, and further revisions, if necessary. In applying strategic planning, the total organization and its several parts are held accountable for reaching the goals. As these management procedures are becoming more widely known, they are frequently being recommended by businessmen and other laymen for use in schools. Some boards of education are seizing upon the concept of responsibility for attaining goals and the companion concept of accountability as the proper bases for guiding sustained efforts to improve education.

These three recent developments appear to be important factors in the sudden emphasis being given throughout the nation to the word *accountability*. But because the attention given to it arises from different backgrounds, there is no single model of accountability presented in current discussions. This is evident in the articles and excerpts which are presented in this book.

Issues

In the discussions and debates over educational accountability, several major issues have emerged. One questions the propriety or even the right of the lay public to ask for evidence of the effectiveness of the work of professionals. There is a long tradition that professionals, especially the clergy, physicians, and lawyers work from a body of doctrine that cannot be understood by the layman; hence laymen are not able to appraise their work. Questions of competence or of malpractice should be decided by the judgment of other professionals. Following this tradition, the work of teachers is sometimes treated as a professional activity, not capable of being understood by laymen. Some argue that it is not proper, perhaps not even right, for the lay public to ask professional educators for an accounting of the results of their work.

On the other hand, some assert that the schools are supported as a service to the public and the public has the right to demand an accounting. Which children are learning and which are not? What are they learning? How much are they learning? It is an obligation, this argument runs, for boards of education and legislators, to obtain and make public the results of systematic, unbiased, reliable appraisals of the results being attained by the schools.

A second issue relates to the learning goals for which schools are accountable. Parents of disadvantaged children emphasize the goals of reading comprehension, arithmetic computation and problem solving, and saleable occupational skills as the important results for which the schools should be accountable. In their demands, little or nothing is said about art, music, science, and the social studies. The more articulate taxpayers' organizations mention reading, arithmetic, occupational skills, and respect for law and order as the goals for which they would hold schools accountable. These are only a part of the educational objectives which most schools have set for themselves. Many educators maintain that a program of accountability that appraises the results of the school's efforts only in a few fields of instruction would focus the efforts of teachers and pupils solely upon these areas to the neglect of the rest of the school objectives.

A third issue has to do with whose responsibility it is to set the goals for which a school will be held accountable. To many laymen, unfamiliar with the wide range of individual differences in the educational backgrounds of school children, and not knowing the limitations of test norms, the setting of goals seems almost automatic. They state it simply: "Every child should make one year's progress in one year. If some children do not make a year's progress in that year, the school, to that extent, has failed to meet its obligation."

On the other hand, teachers point out that some children have much more difficulty in school than others so that the effort required and the guidance needed will vary greatly depending on the backgrounds of the children in each classroom. Furthermore, a test norm represents the average achievement of a representative sample of pupils. Usually half of the sample receives higher scores and half lower scores. A year's progress as indicated by test scores is a figure obtained by subtracting the mean score of pupils in one grade from the mean score of the pupils in the grade above. It does not represent any actual measure of the progress made by individual pupils from one year to the next. So the setting of goals is not the simple, nearly automatic, step that some laymen have supposed.

Others have explained that when goals are established for production or for sales in a business organization, the people involved participate in the goal setting. If they do not believe the goals to be attainable, they cannot be expected to work hard to achieve them. On this ground, it is argued, that within each school, teachers, parents, and perhaps others, should review the information available about the educational backgrounds and previous achievements of each class and goals be established that are both desirable and attainable as viewed by the teachers concerned as well as the parents.

A fourth issue is the means by which the attainment of goals is to be measured. In the past, many schools have reported to the public the results of standard achievement tests, and these have been treated as though they were valid and reliable measures of the attainment by the pupils of the goals of the school. The limitations of standard achievement tests for this purpose are now being widely recognized. They do not measure what the pupil has learned but rather where he stands on a scale that arranges those who have taken the test from the highest score to the lowest. They do not furnish an adequate sample of exercises for the reliable measurement of the upper and lower thirds of school children. Accountability for pupil learning is more dependably assessed by criterion-referenced tests, but there are few of them thus far available. What measures can presently be used is a question being warmly debated.

A fifth issue arises from different views about the range of persons who should be held accountable for the educational results of the school. Some see the effectiveness of a pupil's learning as almost solely the result of the efforts of his teachers. Hence, to them, the teachers are the sole responsible agents and should be held accountable for attaining the educational goals of the school. However, there is a great deal of research evidence to show that the school learning of children is related to a number of factors in addition to the work of the teacher. The school principal is a major influence on the morale and the ways of working of the teachers, the central administration establishes curriculum guidelines and many other policies that affect the work of the teacher. The board of education is responsible for the allocation of resources to the schools. The public's support of taxation influences the level of resources to be allocated to the schools, and its attitude toward various educational goals influences both teachers and pupils. The home environment and the examples of the child's playmates and reference groups powerfully influence his school learning. With these facts in mind, some maintain that a comprehensive system of accountability will identify the positive and negative contributions of all these major influences on pupil learning rather than to single out the teachers or the professional staff in allocating praise or blame. They would involve all of these groups in serious planning for improved education and expect each group to give of its time and energy to doing its part in future educational developments.

A final issue in current debates is that of the use of accountability procedures. On the one hand are those who would announce that the schools are being held accountable for definite educational goals, and when the appraisal indicated that these goals are not being met in certain schools or classrooms, the responsible administrators would be discharged because of their failure to manage their part of the school system in a way that brought results. New administrators would be employed and they would be expected to diagnose the previous failures and to redesign the learning plan and, where appropriate, reassign teachers so as to obtain an effective school—effective in reaching the goals for which it is accountable. This seems to many to be a model of the effective and efficient business operation that could be helpfully used in schools.

Brushing aside the fact that this is not an accurate description of effective business practice, it is clear that teachers are not employees who simply do what they are told. Teachers are motivated by a belief in what they are teaching and their confidence that they can help children learn. They are guided by the model in their minds of how children learn and how teachers can help them learn. If teachers are to change their ways of working, they must understand what better they can do and how to do it. They must really believe in the new ways. Those who have this view of teaching argue for the use of accountability procedures to inform the teachers, the parents, the interested public as well as pupils themselves, about desirable educational goals, about the extent of their attainment, about the problems identified. Accountability procedures should encourage wide cooperation in attacking these problems in an informed and intelligent way. Those who argue for this use, see accountability as an aid to understanding the school situations and one basis for guiding new plans and efforts. There are, of course, several other views about uses. Some would argue for more limited or more extensive uses of accountability procedures. This is clearly an issue of active controversy.

These six issues are not the only ones that can be identified in the present debates, but they are among the chief ones. Although accountability has become a major subject of educational discussion, the issues have not been resolved and several remain to be clarified. The purpose of this book is to present some of the current proposals, discussion, and debate to furnish a background for further study and resolution of issues.

II

Accountability
for Results:
A Basic Challenge
for America's Schools

Leon M. Lessinger

Today, too many young Americans leave school without the tools of learning, an interest in learning, or any idea of the relationships of learning to jobs. It is a mocking challenge that so many of our children are not being reached today by the very institution charged with the primary responsibility for teaching them. A Committee for Economic Development report issued in the summer of 1968 summarizes the indictment: Many schools and school districts, handicapped by outmoded organization and a lack of research and development money, are not providing "the kind of education that produces rational, responsible, and effective citizens."

Now, the educational establishment—right down to the local level—is being asked ever more insistently to account for the results of its programs. This fast-generating nation-wide demand for accountability promises a major and long overdue redevelopment of the management of the present educational system, including an overhaul of its cottage-industry form of organization. Many believe this can be accomplished by making use of modern techniques currently employed in business and industry, some of which are already being used in the educational enterprise.

Before America's schools can productively manage the massive amount of money entrusted to them—and the even greater amount they need—they must be armed with better management capability. If education is going to be able to manage its budget properly, it must devise measurable relationships between dollars spent and results obtained. Education, like industry, requires a system of quality assurance. Anything less will shortchange our youth.

Quality Assurance

Sputniks and satellite cities, computers and confrontation politics, television and the technology of laborsaving devices—all have placed new and overwhelming demands on our educational system. Americans could say with the angel Gabriel of the play, *The Green Pastures*, that "everything nailed down is coming loose." How can we provide the kind of education that would assure full participation for all in this new, complex, technological society? How to prepare people to respond creatively to rapid-fire change all their lives while maintaining a personal identity that would give them and their society purpose and direction? How to do this when the body of knowledge has so exploded that it no longer can be stored in a single mind? How to do this when cybernetics is changing man's functions? How to do this when the cost of old-fashioned education soars higher every year with little significant improvement?

In 1965, the passage of the far-reaching Elementary and Secondary Education Act gave the public schools of America a clear new mandate and some of the funds to carry it out. It was a mandate not just for equality of educational opportunity but for equity in results as well. In place of the old screening, sorting, and reject system that put students somewhere on a bell-shaped curve stretching from A to F, the schools were asked to bring educational benefits to every young person to prepare him for a productive life. Under the new mandate the schools were expected to give every pupil the basic competence he needed, regardless of his so-called ability, interest, background, home, or income. After all, said a concerned nation, what's the purpose of grading a basic skill like reading with A, B, C, D, or F when you can't make it at all today if you can't read?

In essence, this meant that education would be expected to develop a "zero reject system" which would guarantee quality in skill acquisition just as a similar system now guarantees the quality of industrial production. Today's diplomas are often meaningless warranties. In the words of one insistent inner-city parent, "Many diplomas aren't worth the ink they're written in." We know, for example, that there are some 30,000 functional illiterates—people with less than fifth grade reading ability—in the country today who hold diplomas. And untold more are uncovered each day as manpower training and job programs bring increasing numbers of hard-core unemployed into the labor market.

Instead of certifying that a student has spent so much time in school or taken so many courses, the schools should be certifying that he is able to perform specific tasks. Just as a warranty certifies the quality performance of a car, a diploma should certify a youngster's performance as a reader, a writer, a driver, and so on.

If, then, the new objective of education is to have zero rejects through basic competence for all, how can the educational establishment retool to respond to this new challenge? Developing a system of quality assurance can help provide the way.

A Plan for Educational Redevelopment

The first step toward such a system is to draw up an overall educational redevelopment plan. Such a plan must first translate the general goal of competence for all students into a school district's specific objectives. These objectives must be formulated in terms of programs, courses, buildings, curriculums, materials, hardware, personnel, and budgets. The plan must incorporate a timetable of priorities for one year, for five years, ten years, and perhaps even for twenty years. Such a plan should be based on "market research," that is, an investigation of the needs of the students in each particular school. It should also be based on research and development to facilitate constant updating of specifications to meet these needs. Through the plan, the school district would be able to measure its own output against the way its students actually perform. It would be able to see exactly what results flow from the dollars it has invested.

The purpose of the educational redevelopment plan, of course, is to provide a systematic approach for making the changes in educational organization and practice necessitated by the new demands on the education system. To assure that the plan will provide quality, it should use a combination of measurements that are relevant, reliable, objective, easily assessable, and that produce data in a form that can be processed by modern-day technology. As a further guarantee of quality, teams of school administrators, teachers, and modern educational and technical specialists competent to interpret the results should be available. The plan should also spell out a clear relationship between results and goals, thus providing for accountability.

In reality, this educational plan is only a piece of paper—a set of ideals and a set of step-by-step progressions which schools and districts can approximate. But it does provide a blueprint for the educational managers of the district—the superintendents, teachers, principals, and school boards—who must provide the leadership and the understanding to carry out educational change.

To be effective and to assure that its specifications remain valid, an educational redevelopment plan must set aside dollars for research and development. The Committee for Economic Development in a 1971 report revealed that less than one percent of our total national education investment goes into research and development. "No major industry," the report said, "would expect to progress satisfactorily unless it invested many times that amount in research and development." Many private companies plow as much as 15 per cent of their own funds back into research and development.

If one percent of the yearly budget for education was set aside for research and development, we would have a national educational research and development fund of roughly $500 million. Such money could attract new services, new energies, new partnerships to education. And they would inspire competition that would spur rapid educational development. This research and development money could be used to buy technical assistance, drawing on the expertise of private industry, the nonprofit organizations, the universities, the professions, and the arts. The administrative functions of a school system—construction, purchasing, disbursement, personnel, payroll—also demand business and management skills.

Why not draw on business for technical assistance or actual management in these areas? Or for that matter, in formulating the educational redevelopment plan itself? The final step in setting up a quality assurance system is providing for accountability of both the educational process and its products, the students. Do pupils meet the overall objectives and the performance specifications that the school considers essential? Can Johnny read, write, figure? Can he also reason? Can he figure out where to find a given piece of information not necessarily stored in his head? Does he understand enough about himself and our society to have pride in his culture, a sureness about his own personal goals and identity, as well as an understanding of his responsibilities to society? Does he have the various cognitive and social skills to enter a wide range of beginning jobs and advance in the job market?

The Technology of Teaching

The accountability of process, of classroom practice, is somewhat harder to get at. At the risk of mixing it up with ideas about educational hardware, we might call it the technology of teaching. To find out a little about it, we might start by asking whether things are being done differently today in a particular classroom than they were done in the past.

A host of disenchanted teachers and others—from Bel Kaufman in her book *Up the Down Staircase* to Jonathan Kozol in *Death at an Early Age*—have been telling us over the past few years what has been happening up to now in many classrooms in America. In *The Way It Spozed to Be*,* James Herndon, a California school-teacher, describes one kind of advice he got from experienced teachers during his first year in an inner-city school as a conglomeration of tricks, dodges, and gimmicks to get the students to do what they were "spozed" to do. The purpose of the methods used was to get and keep order so that "learning could take place."

Today, teachers often try to teach order, responsibility, citizenship, or punctuality, while believing that they are teaching reading or French or gym. If Johnny forgets his pencil, for example, he actually may not be permitted to take the French quiz and might get an F—presumably for forgetfulness, certainly not for French, for the grade does not reflect Johnny's competence in French.

In one state's schools, girls' physical education regularly chalks up far more F's than any other course. A study of the reasons indicated that gym teachers actually were attempting to measure citizenship by tallying whether Jane kept a dirty locker or failed to take a shower. The grade hardly reflected her competence in physical education. Requirements such as punctuality, neatness, order, and time served ought not to be used to reflect school subject mastery.

Despite considerable evidence to the contrary, many schools and teachers are still grouping youngsters as good or bad raw material. What can you do with bad raw material? some teachers ask, much as some doctors once asked about the mentally ill. What we are searching for in place of a "demonology" of teaching is sensitive and sensible classroom practice—a practice that treats every child as a person and uses a variety of pleasurable techniques to improve his performance in anticipated and replicable ways. We are not sure this will result in more learning—though we think it will—but we do know that sensitive and sensible classroom practice is good in itself. As such it will pay off in human ways, even if it doesn't pay off in learning.

As teachers' salaries rise and their demands for rights and benefits are rightfully met by the communities they serve, those communities can expect that teacher responsibility will also grow.

---

*James Herndon, *The Way It Spozed to Be* (New York: Simon & Schuster, Inc., 1968).

In fact, they can insist on it. They can insist that better pay, more rights, and more status bring with them better standard practice in the schools and classrooms. They can insist that teachers become accountable for relating process and procedures to results. And pupil accomplishment, though it may reflect some new hardware and construction, by and large reflects teacher and administrator growth and development. This is the true meaning of a new technology of teaching.

Educational Audits

Thus the changes that result when the redevelopment plan has been carried out must be demonstrably apparent in terms of both teacher and pupil progress. In order to measure how these actual results compare with the detailed objectives of the plan, it makes sense to call for an outside educational audit, much like the outside fiscal audit required of every school system today. The school system could request an audit either of its overall program or of specific parts of that program.

This new approach could conceivably lead to the establishment of a new category of certified educational auditors whose principal job would be to visit school districts, on invitation, to help determine the success of local program planning in achieving prestated goals. One expert suggests that an educational audit need take only 10 school days a year for a single school system. His idea is to send a completely equipped and staffed mobile educational audit van to visit about 20 school systems a year.

Educators should also be encouraged to describe and measure the behavior expected of each student upon completion of programs funded from federal sources. To reinforce accountability for results, contracts for federal funds might be written as performance agreements. Thus a proposal for funds to back a reading program might stipulate that 90 percent of the participating students would be able to satisfy criteria by demonstrating they had achieved a particular advance in grade level in the time proposed.

Furthermore, special financial incentives based on meeting performance criteria might be specified in these contracts. For example, a certain amount of dollars might be awarded to a school for each student who achieves a high school diploma (defined as a verification that 16 credits have been attained in specific subjects with a credit defined as 72 hours of successful classroom study). Or a school might be given monetary awards for each student who has been employed for a year after leaving the institution.

Performance Contracts

Lest the idea of performance contracts strike anyone as novel or bordering upon the impossible, it should be pointed out that they have been formulated and applied with great success by both industry and the armed services for years. The fact that many results of education are subjective and not subject to audit should not stop us from dealing precisely with those aspects that do lend themselves to definition and assessment.

Directors of ESEA projects should have training in how to manage large sums of money. Running half-million and million-dollar programs takes considerable expertise in management. Obviously, managers of these projects need technical assistance if they are to manage in the best and most modern sense. For example, there should be technical reviews of all successful programs, practices, and materials used in embryo experimental projects. Educational objectives should be translated into a clearer framework for the purposes of reporting, evaluation, and feedback. In most cases, schools would need outside technical assistance to carry out either of these tasks.

Greater educational management competence is also needed in an area that might be called "educational logistics." Many projects do not get off the ground because the equipment, personnel, and training they depend upon are not properly coordinated. The notion of staging, for example, to bring together all the elements that are necessary for a project to achieve performance is very important. Virtually the only time you see this, in education in general as well as in ESEA projects, is in selected activities.

Path to Citizenship

Today formal education is the chief path to full citizenship. School credits and diplomas and licenses are milestones on that path. Schooling is literally the bridge—or the barrier—between a man and his ability to earn his bread. Without it a citizen is condemned to economic obsolescence almost before he begins to work.

If we accept competence for all as one of the major goals of education today, then we must devise a system of accountability that relates education's vast budget to results. It is a paradox that while our technologically oriented society is a masterful producer of the artifacts our civilization needs, it seems incapable of applying that technology to educating our young citizens.

We can change the way our educational system performs so that the desired result—a competently trained young citizenry—

becomes the focus of the entire process. In the same way that planning, market studies, research and development, and performance warranties determine industrial production and its worth to consumers, so should we be able to engineer, organize, refine, and manage the educational system to prepare students to contribute to the most complex and exciting country on earth.

III

Official Endorsements
of Accountability

Increasingly, the notion of accountability has figured in the management of educational programs undertaken by federal and state agencies. Two states, Florida and Colorado, have in recent months passed legislation providing for educational accountability and other states are considering similar moves.

In this section we include a portion of President Nixon's Message to Congress on Education Reform (March 3, 1970) in which the President endorsed the concept of accountability.

At the meeting of the Education Commission of the States in Denver in July, 1970, the theme of accountability was a prominent one. A number of statements were made illustrating the interest of state officials in the concept. We have reprinted here the remarks made on that occasion by Governor William G. Milliken of Michigan, Governor Russell W. Peterson of Delaware, and Dr. Ewald B. Nyquist, New York Commissioner of Education and President of the University of the State of New York. The speeches appeared in *Compact* magazine, Volume 4, October, 1970, published by the Education Commission of the States, Denver, Colorado.

From a Message to Congress
in Education Reform

President Richard M. Nixon

What makes a "good" school? The old answer was a school that maintained high standards of plant and equipment; that had a reasonable number of children per classroom; whose teachers had

15

good college and often graduate training; a school that kept up to date with new curriculum developments, and was alert to new techniques in instruction. This was a fair enough definition so long as it was assumed that there was a direct connection between these "school characteristics" and the actual amount of learning that takes place in a school.

Years of educational research, culminating in the Equal Opportunity Survey of 1966 have, however, demonstrated that this direct, uncomplicated relationship does not exist.

Apart from the general public interest in providing teachers an honorable and well paid professional career, there is only one important question to be asked about education: *What do the children learn?*

Unfortunately, it is simply not possible to make any confident deduction from school characteristics as to what will be happening to the children in any particular school. Fine new buildings alone do not predict high achievement. Pupil-teacher ratios may not make as much difference as we used to think. Expensive equipment may not make as much difference as its salesmen would have us believe.

And yet we know that something does make a difference.

The *outcome* of schooling—what children learn—is profoundly different for different groups of children and different parts of the country. Although we do not seem to understand just what it is in one school or school system that produces a different outcome from another, one conclusion is inescapable: *We do not yet have equal educational opportunity in America.*

The purpose of the National Institute of Education would be to begin the serious, systematic search for new knowledge needed to make educational opportunity truly equal.

The corresponding need in the school systems of the nation is to begin the responsible, open measurement of how well the educational process is working. It matters very little how much a school building costs; it matters a great deal how much a child in that building learns. An important beginning in measuring the end result of education has already been made through the National Assessment of Educational Progress being conducted by the Education Commission of the States.

To achieve this fundamental reform it will be necessary to develop broader and more sensitive measurements of learning than we now have.

The National Institute of Education would take the lead in developing these new measurements of educational output. In doing so it should pay as much heed to what are called the "immeasurables" of schooling (largely because no one has yet learned to measure them) such as responsibility, wit and humanity as it does to verbal and mathematical achievement.

In developing these new measurements, we will want to begin by comparing the actual educational effectiveness of schools in similar economic and geographic circumstances. We will want to be alert to the fact that in our present educational system we will often find our most devoted, most talented, hardest working teachers in those very schools where the general level of achievement is lowest. They are often there because their commitment to their profession sends them where the demands upon their profession are the greatest.

From these considerations we derive another new concept: *Accountability*. School administrators and school teachers alike are responsible for their performance, and it is in their interest as well as in the interests of their pupils that they be held accountable. Success should be measured not by some fixed national norm, but rather by the results achieved in relation to the actual situation of the particular school and the particular set of pupils.

For years the fear of "national standards" has been one of the bugaboos of education. There has never been any serious effort to impose national standards on educational programs, and if we act wisely in this generation we can be reasonably confident that no such effort will arise in future generations. The problem is that in opposing some mythical threat of "national standards" what we have too often been doing is avoiding accountability for our own local performance. We have, as a nation, too long avoided thinking of the *productivity* of schools.

This is a mistake because it undermines the principle of local control of education. Ironic though it is, the avoidance of accountability is the single most serious threat to a continued, and even more pluralistic educational system. Unless the local community can obtain dependable measures of just how well its school system is performing for its children, the demand for national standards will become even greater and in the end almost certainly will prevail. When local officials do not respond to a real local need, the search begins for a level of officialdom that will do so, and all too often in the past this search has ended in Washington.

I am determined to see to it that the flow of power in education goes toward, and not away from the local community. The diversity and freedom of education in this nation, founded on local administration and State responsibility, must prevail.

Making the School System Accountable

William G. Milliken

What do we mean by accountability? Accountability can mean a strict accounting by educators for the ways in which they spend money or an accurate means of testing how effectively educators are teaching children or any one of several other possible meanings.

Whatever accountability means to each of us individually, I think we hold in common a collective sense of its implications. And the chief implication is that people are increasingly demanding to know how their children are learning, what they are learning, and why they are being taught whatever they are being taught.

To create confidence where little or no confidence exists is the principal task of American education today. We cannot create this confidence by reciting a litany of accomplishments . . . all the money we are spending, all of the schools we are building, all of the new programs we have initiated. We can only create, or recreate, this confidence by eliminating our failures.

The best opportunity we have to create new confidence in public education is to expand the role of the states in the field of education. I believe that this can be done without diminishing local control of the schools. As a matter of fact, I believe if the states meet their responsibilities in education, local school officials will be able to do a better job.

As many . . . [people] know, I submitted a far-reaching program of educational reform to the Michigan Legislature last Fall (1969).

The major elements of the plan have not yet become law. But I will continue fighting for this plan as long as I am Governor. For I believe that without bold and sweeping reform in finance and administration, there can be no significant increase in the quality of American education.

Proposals for Reform   The program proposes replacing intermediate districts with regional education centers. These intermediate districts (there are sixty of them in Michigan) now float in semi-autonomous limbo between the state and local school districts. We are convinced that replacing them with regional centers would vastly improve the delivery of such services as special education, vocational education and a variety of administrative responsibilities.

Second, in order to develop a more rational administrative structure, I have proposed a new system in which the Governor would appoint the state superintendent of public instruction, with the advice and consent of the Senate. The qualifications for the director would be spelled out in law, so that there would be no chance of a purely political appointment. In any event, the performance of the department and the superintendent would be the direct responsibility of the Governor. The Governor would be held accountable for the performance of the department, and the people would have a chance to make a judgment at the ballot box.

Third, school financing. I do not have to remind [you] . . . how difficult it is to apply the concept of accountability to educational financing. I think all of us would like to finance schools and colleges on the basis of proven pupil achievement. But we cannot agree on a definition of learning, nor am I sure that we should. Financing reform is at the heart of proposals that I have submitted to the people of Michigan.

The most significant statement on state responsibility in the area of school financing was made . . . . two years ago by Dr. James B. Conant. Largely on the basis of Dr. Conant's arguments, I became convinced that most of the responsibility for financing elementary and secondary education should be transferred to the states.

Dr. Conant has proposed that all authority to levy taxes for schools at the local level be eliminated and that the local share of school financing be taken over by the states. My proposals do not go as far as those of Dr. Conant and others. But they do move significantly in the same direction.

Specifically, the program which I have submitted calls for a uniform and limited property tax for school operations. This tax, which would require a constitutional amendment, would equalize the property tax burden. The total property tax levied throughout the state would be decreased substantially, and the state income tax would be increased to offset the cut in tax on property.

I believe that the distribution of funds to local districts should be related directly to need. My proposals recognize the varying need among districts—special needs for vocational and special education and the needs of under-achieving students. In addition, the budgeting process provided in my program would recognize differences in educational costs throughout the state.

Assessment in Michigan   Finally, accountability in the sense of accomplishment, what the students learn, and how to measure it. In this regard, Michigan, like the Education Commission of the States, has embarked on a program of educational assessment, which I have supported strongly. Much more work needs to be done in the area of educational assessment, for until the measurement of educational progress can be clearly defined, we will be unable to develop a system for correcting educational deficiencies which have been revealed.

The fact that less than one percent of our total national education investment goes into research and development is indefensible. The federal government has made some important new commitments in educational research and development. President Nixon's National Institute of Education is one of the most exciting programs in national education policy in recent years. Recognizing this need at the state level, I am presently considering the establishment of an educational research and development organization in Michigan, combining the expertise of state government, the universities and the private sector.

We live in a time of multiple crises, and no approach to the solution of these crises is as promising as education. The quality of American education must be raised if we are to survive the Twentieth Century. Somehow, in the process, we must give our young people something more than the technical skills to earn a living. We must give them respect for the past, confidence in the present and a faith in the future.

We must introduce into the American education system a spiritual dimension which it does not now possess. We must show young people all along the line that we regard them as individuals—not to be folded, mutilated or spindled by an educational establishment which treats them as products instead of human beings.

Our goals cannot be reached by the federal government alone, or by the state governments alone, or by local school districts alone. They will only be reached by all units of government working together in creative partnership. And the time has come for state government to be something more than a silent partner.

Accountability in Elementary and Secondary Education

Russell W. Peterson

Accountability as a State Function.   There is no doubt that accountability is the most important of the state's functions in terms of need, opportunity and cost. State governments and their agencies such as local school districts provide services to people. Many of the state's services can be fairly easily measured. For instance, the number of miles of highway built or rebuilt can be counted along with the number of people using the roads. We have automated monitors to record pollutant concentrations which tell us how effective pollution control is. In crime, even though it is more difficult, we do have statistical measures of performance.

I have set out specific output goals for Delaware state agencies over the next one to ten years. Some examples are: Reducing the amount of violent crime 25 percent by 1976, 50 percent by 1980. Getting 1,000 welfare recipients off the rolls and into jobs by a specified date. Having Delaware, within five years, lead the nation with the lowest number of deaths and injuries per automobile passenger mile. As Governor, I am accountable for achievement of these specific goals.

I winced a little in reviewing my objectives for education. All the goals are inputs, such as: completing the institution of state-supported kindergartens, making all schools in Delaware community schools, completing the upgrading of occupational-vocational education in all high schools and establishing prekindergarten programs for all four-year-olds by 1976.

Why couldn't I have listed as goals for education such things as: reducing high school dropouts by 50 percent; insuring that every child who left the schools could read and comprehend political and economic news, so that he could function effectively as a literate voter; reducing to less than three percent the number of kids graduating from high school who are racially prejudiced by 1976 when we will celebrate the 200th Anniversary of our Declaration of Independence?

Educators traditionally think in terms of inputs—new programs, more dollars for materials, higher teacher salaries, and the like. We have files, and wastebaskets, full of statistics about education—how many schools, how many teachers, how many strikes and campus rebellions.

In principle, the American educational commitment has been that every child should have an adequate education. This commitment has been stated in terms of resources such as teachers, books, space and equipment. In fact, most of the outside accreditation techniques for elementary and secondary education still use measures of input as prime criteria for performance.

When a child fails to learn, school personnel have all too often labeled him "slow," "unmotivated" or "retarded." Our schools must assume the commitment that every child shall learn. Such a commitment must include the willingness to change a system that does not work, or to find one that does; to seek causes of failure in the system and its personnel, instead of entirely in students.

Let us adopt Lessinger's definition of accountability. That is, "Holding the school accountable for results in terms of student learning rather than solely in the use of input resources."

<u>Underlying Concepts</u> From the acknowledged prejudices of my scientific and industrial background, let me share with you some concepts in accountability.

First, most pupil achievement in elementary and secondary education can be measured. Second is the importance of detailed, measurable educational objectives. Third is the necessity for evaluation by the independent accomplishment audit procedure. Fourth, the absolute necessity for complete, unvarnished performance feedback to the decision-makers. Finally, a real commitment "that every child shall learn."

Let's talk about measurement. The common cry from educators, particularly those working with disadvantaged children, is that education is too intangible to be measured. There are many methods of assessment, and teachers should specify the method of measuring what the student has learned. It does not have to involve standardized testing.

Very important is the establishment of detailed, measurable educational objectives. Even those educators who cry "It can't be measured" must admit that we teach with the notion that there is something to be learned. It is absolutely essential that a detailed list of concepts, skills and attitudes for each learning unit be set out in advance. The objective must be stated in measurable terms and should specify the method of evaluating whether the concept has been learned.

I would like to stress the necessity of independently evaluating results by using independent accomplishment audits. We want to evaluate results, not inputs. Results are the products, services or other effects created by the school. Results stand in contrast to resources consumed by the school.

Next, but very important, we must talk about the evaluation or audit process which can be an important stimulus to accountability. To be effective, the audit must be based on the objectives of the course or program as developed by the staff, students or even the community. The objectives must be specific and the auditor must agree with the program people on the method of measuring whether the locally developed objectives have been met.

The next point covers a fundamental of all systems—feedback. The continuing reluctance of professional educators to allow the newspapers to publish comparative standardized achievement test scores for examination by the citizens is a real problem. The newspapers contend that it is public information. The educators say that publishing comparative test scores will give misinformation because results do not indicate the inherent capability of the students. This argument must be resolved; indeed, it has been resolved in some large cities by publishing of test scores along with other socio-economic indicators of inherent pupil ability.

I am less concerned with whether newspapers publish test scores than whether or not the lay citizens who set the educational priorities and allocate funds are getting proper feedback. It is imperative that these decision-makers get all the facts—good and bad, pleasant or disquieting.

Commitment   Someone has stated that in America education has become our God. This is a general mystical belief—a blind faith that somehow education will solve all our problems.

I am for the commitment to education. But not the blind faith of some professional educators who say just give us more dollars, let us alone and we'll get the job done. We have been doing pretty much that and the evidence is pretty conclusive: We are making headway but the job is not getting done for many of the children in our society.

How do we get started in making teachers and administrators accountable for results? First, local school boards, with their professional educational leaders, must make a commitment that each child will accomplish one specified increment of learning for each period of attendance in the school district. The economists would call this accountability for the value added during each year of education. This is the ultimate in accountability.

What are we going to do about the children who don't achieve? It will take much more individual testing, special programs of remediation, summer schools, programs for children with learning disabilities and many more. Sure it will. But some states, like Delaware, have stated legislative policy that "the State Board of Education and local school districts shall provide special classes and facilities to meet the needs of all handicapped, gifted and talented children." In any case, it will be far easier to sell programs to assist children who are lagging if the district has agreed to be accountable for results.

It is well known that individuals, teams, business organizations and governmental agencies achieve considerably more when they are being held accountable for specific, measurable goals. This is particularly true when the goals have been set by individuals in the organization through participative management.

Now is the time when professional educators and key lay decision-makers must make a commitment to deliver on one of the most radical ideas in history—allowing every child in America to develop to the limit of his ability.

Measuring Purposes and Effectiveness

Ewald B. Nyquist

Evaluation essentially has to do with finding out how successful an educational activity has been. It means, too, comparing the costs employed in an activity with the benefits obtained from it.

Evaluation also means cost effectiveness analyses designed to measure the extent to which resources allocated to a specific objective under each of several alternatives actually contribute to accomplishing that objective. Finally, evaluation implies precise program goals and educational objectives stated in behavioral terms and measurable operational terms. Evaluation techniques can be both objective and subjective in education, for not everything in education can be scientifically determined.

Accountability means, to me, the continuous willingness to evaluate education, to explain and interpret the results with all candor and divulge the results to the public or constituencies that need to know them, and to be personally and organizationally responsible for the weaknesses as well as the strengths revealed.

Growing Pressures   Coupled with increased funds for education, there has been a growing recognition that legislators and taxpayers have a considerably heightened interest in the increased educational effectiveness and quality which the added funds are supposed to produce.

Is there any school system that has not experienced in recent years increased demands, sometimes emotional, from parents, school boards, taxpayers or legislators, for evidence that they are getting their money's worth, or conversely, sharp criticisms that the education being provided is not good enough?

And the pressures are increasing. We can expect sharply increased demands for accountability from the parents of those children we have been less successful in educating. Teachers, in their mood of aggressive militancy, are going to make demands on their conditions of employment which will bear positively on increasing education effectiveness, and, as in New York City today, to make contract terms pledging themselves responsible as well.

Students are asking for accountability. They are questioning the accuracy of the curriculum, its meaningfulness for them. They are sharply questioning the whole concept of teacher tenure, and they are criticizing the antiquated school policies, paternalistic methods of governance and the inadequacies of sandbox student government. And federal and state legislators are setting precedents by mandating evaluation in increasingly precise terms, calling for hard-nosed performance data.

Administrators and school board members and state education departments are in the middle and are in for more trying times than they have yet seen.

There are two aspects to accountability: Have the funds been spent for the purpose intended; and what effective use has been made of them?

No one can protest that one should be held fiscally accountable for money received and spent. Educators and school boards, because they deal with a largely intangible product, are not quite as used, as others are, to providing a full reckoning for funds received.

There is an accelerating public demand for accounting of our educational stewardship. Evaluation has become one of the major challenges to education in this decade. What it means is that school boards and local and state educators will face the responsibility of taking the public into full partnership, explaining the problems and limitations of testing and other means of evaluating education, welcoming assistance and sharing the resulting information.

Possible Measurements I firmly believe, for one thing, that in order to let people know the quality of the return on their educational investment, an annual report of school achievement, including test results should be made to the community. Such a report could include follow-up information on graduates, changes in pupil achievement, new types of testing that are being tried, characteristics of the student body being served, and comparisons with other appropriate school systems and statewide standards.

I believe in publicized honesty. We have not done a good job of interpreting to the public what kind of an educational job we are doing and in providing the evidence that the educational system is doing what is expected of it.

Many aspects of education are intangible and subjective and do not lend themselves to a bloodless scientific appraisal. Take creativity, self-image, the tone of a school. And we need to remind ourselves that there are many conditions in the schools that are not conducive to learning, for which there is a collective responsibility. Let us not put the whole burden on the schools. Responsibility for poor housing, poverty, unemployment, adult prejudice, and urban decay lies elsewhere. Accountability is interlocking among many partners.

It has been estimated that no more than five percent, if that, of the schools in America have any sound demonstrable knowledge about the effects of the impact of the various aspects of their educational enterprises and efforts on the students. That is, they do not know how much the students have learned because of what the schools have done, or in spite of what they have done.

I am not interested in using evaluation systems or instruments to fix blame nor to punish teachers or administrators, nor to withhold funds from school districts, but rather to detect weaknesses and find solutions for them.

Providing an increased educational accountability to the public will require new attitudes, new techniques, imagination, a willingness to experiment with boldness, greater flexibility, innovation and money.

Accountability requires the measurement of both educational output and resource input. The definition of cost should be such as to make possible comparisons across state lines as well as across school district lines.

Furthermore, the future of accountability requires more than just the purification of measures of quality and costs. Units of measurement should be such that the change in each can be assessed. For instance, we should be able eventually with assurance to say that an increase of $20 per pupil for reading will increase reading achievement by two school months in the fourth grade. That is actually a term in a performance contract.

Cost accounting must become operative in schools. Procedures for estimating the cost of various programs are available, although require a certain amount of "guesstimating."

Performance contracting and the voucher system seem to be promising developments in providing increased accountability. I believe also in establishing a creative interplay with private enterprise.

Existing evaluation instruments and methods do not uniformly tell us whether we are doing as well as we should be doing in the teaching and learning process given the intellectual capacities of our students, the level of competence in the staff, surrounding social and economic conditions, and the educational resources available.

Most instruments provide standards that are normative, as the phrase goes; that is, allowing schools to compare themselves with each other or pupils with each other. We do not have adequate instruments of educational expectancy in view of school and pupil resources and conditions, based not on what other schools have achieved but on what schools with such resources and conditions ought to receive. The National Assessment Program will only give us an inventory of knowledge. It will not tell us what we ought to be achieving, given the fiscal inputs in human resources.

Who should be responsible for evaluation, and who is to be held accountable? Everybody, of course—local school systems, colleges and universities, states, and the federal government, with the states playing a major or primary role.

I have a special comment for the federal government. I say to those in charge, don't expect too much in efficient and meaningful evaluation in educational accountability from the states and local school systems when (a) federally supported educational programs are abruptly begun, ruptured or emasculated altogether, and (b) appropriations for a fiscal year are made after ten months of that year have already elapsed. The dialogue on accountability, to me, must be symmetrical.

I urge expansion of the National Assessment samples within states so that results may be compared with those of the nation, the region, and with other states. I would suggest, too, that the Commission seek out and work with appropriate individuals and organizations in an effort to cost out specific programs in the schools.

IV

Engineering
Accountability
for Results
in Public Education

Leon Lessinger

An important change has taken place in what Americans expect of their public schools. The optimism about the value of education is still there and continues to be strong, but serious doubts have arisen about the public school system's ability to actually deliver on its promises.

The shift in attitude becomes apparent through analysis of the questions being asked at hearings by elected officials of both parties at every level of government, from Congress to state legislatures and local city councils. The same line of questioning can be heard among businessmen, at school board conventions, at various meetings of citizens' groups, and in the highest circles of the executive branches of government. Seekers of educational funds have always talked in terms of books, staff, materials, equipment, and space to be acquired or used, together with students to be served and programs to be offered. Questioners in the past were content to listen to accounts of resources allocated. This has changed. Today the questions focus on results obtained for resources used. The questions are pointed, insistent, and abrasive. The public school system is being held accountable for results. Accountability is the coming *sine qua non* for education in the 1970's. How to engineer accountability for results in public education is the central problem for the education profession.

It would be interesting to speculate about the reasons for the growing demand to link dollars spent for education to results achieved from students. Increased and accelerating costs, poor academic performance of minority children, and inconclusive results of federal compensatory education projects (totaling, since 1965, in the billions of dollars) are probably important causal factors.

Accountability is the product of a process. At its most basic level, it means that an agent, public or private, entering into a contractual agreement to perform a service will be held answerable for performing according to agreed-upon terms, within an established time period, and with a stipulated use of resources and performance standards. This definition of accountability requires that the parties to the contract keep clear and complete records and that this information be available for outside review. It also suggests penalties and rewards; accountability without redress or incentive is mere rhetoric.

Performance contracting is *one* process for which accountability is the product. The idea of contracting is older than free enterprise. Its appeal to both liberals and conservatives revolves around its attention to two things that leaders agree are desperately needed in education—quality assurance and knowledge of results.

At its most primitive level the process works like this: A public authority grants money to a local education agency to contract with private enterprise* to achieve specific goals within specific periods for specific costs. The money is targeted at pressing needs which are not being adequately met, such as dropout prevention among disadvantaged groups or bringing the underpriviledged and undereducated up to competitive educational levels.

Seen from this vantage point, accountability appears to be merely the utilization by education of private enterprise for getting things done. Of course, such utilization is not *per se* a new development. For example, any superintendent of schools can show that performance contracts have long been used in school operation and maintenance. The use of performance contracts to achieve accountability is, therefore, not new to education. It is the extension of this idea into the realm of learning through a particular process, called in this paper educational engineering, which represents what some are calling the "coming revolution in American education."

Since World War II several fields have been developed to enable managers of very complex enterprises to operate efficiently and effectively. These emerging fields of knowledge and practice are commonly known as systems analysis, management by objectives, contract engineering (including bids, warranties, penalties, and incentives), logistics, quality assurance, value engineering, and human factors engineering, to name a few of the more important.

*Performance contracting need not be limited to private enterprise. The principles are applicable for arrangements with teachers, universities, and nonprofit organizations.

If to these are added instructional technology and modern educational management theory, a new and valuable interdisciplinary field emerges. This body of knowledge, skill, and procedure can be called educational engineering. It is the insights from educational engineering that make it possible for performance contracting to achieve accountability for results in education.

Why couple the term "engineering" with education? Why more apparent dehumanization? It is not appropriate here to treat this question at great length. But I note that engineering has traditionally been a problem-solving activity and a profession dedicated to the application of technology to the resolution of real world difficulties and opportunities. While the teaching-learning environment differs from the world of business and industry, some rationalization of the two subcultures may be beneficial. A major objective of educational engineering may very well be to arm educational practitioners with both the technological competence of essential engineering generalizations, strategies, and tools and the professional practice of a successful instructor or educational manager. From this point of view, educational engineering can be a symbiotic art—a marriage of humanism and technology. It is this possible symbiosis that makes performance contracting for learning accomplishment feasible.

Accountability in Operation

The application of one educational engineering process to achieve results in the basic academic skills can be used to illustrate the concept of accountability in operation. This accountability process can be engineered as follows:

1) The local education agency (LEA) employs a management support group (MSG), whose members have competency to assist them in political, social, economic, managerial, and educational matters. The relationship between the management support group and the local school leadership group resembles that of long-term consultants on a retainer account.

2) The MSG works with staff and community (or other groups as required by a particular local situation) to produce a request for proposal (RFP), which is a set of specifications indicating as clearly as possible the service to be performed, the approximate amount of money to be invested, the constraints to be observed, the standards acceptable, and related matters. The RFP is the local education agency's blueprint for action to meet pressing priorities.

3) The next stage of the educational engineering process occurs when the RFP is set out to bid. The pre-bidding conference becomes the forum for educational exchange. Here a rich and varied communication through competition occurs between elements of the private and public sector. The bidding process is flexible to the extent that allowance is made by LEA officials for new insights and better elements to be incorporated into a revised RFP.

4) Following the bidding conference, a revised RFP is issued and actual bids are entertained. The MSG assists the LEA in operating the conference and reviewing the bids. The local board "hears" the top bids in a manner similar to the process used in the employment of an architect.

5) The local school board selects what it considers to be the best bid and enters into negotiation for a performance contract with the successful bidder. The MSG assists at this stage.

6) Concurrently with the signing of the performance contract, an independent educational accomplishment audit team is employed by the LEA both to monitor execution of the performance contract and to provide feedback to the LEA to certify results for purposes of payment.

It may now be helpful to analyze the structural elements of this process in more detail.

The *performance contract* is the managerial tool to assure the achievement of results, while encouraging responsible innovation. The approach is simple in concept although complex in actualization. With technical assistance, the learning problem is analyzed, and a delineation of achievement outcomes to be expected is specified. An RFP is developed and sent by the LEA to potential contractors who have demonstrated competent and creative activity in the specific and related fields. The RFP does not prescribe how the job must be done but does establish the performance, financial, administrative, and legal parameters of the operation. The RFP requires that the bidder guarantee specific results for specific costs. The confidence that the bidder has in his approach is reflected in the level of the guarantee, the social practicability, the time, and the costs indicated in the bid he presents.

The program to be bid, including the specified number of students, is described in the contract. Incentives are provided for the contractor to bring each child up to specified levels of performance, at the lowest cost. Provision is made in the performance contract to develop a program for which the contractor will guarantee results.

After the demonstration period is completed and all relevant costs, procedures, achievements, and performance data have been validated, the contract requires that the contractor guarantee an effective, fiscally responsible program. Then, on a "turnkey" basis, the LEA incorporates the instructional program into the school. Thus performance contracting is a capability-creating resource for public education.

The *management support group* is the catalytic and buffer agency which provides not only technical assistance to the district, but a communication link between those who determine priorities, such as a federal agency, and the school system that is developing program proposals. The group has access to new developments in the field, especially in industrial and governmental sectors, and assists the LEA in developing the RFP to assure that conditions and constraints in the RFP do not preclude but actually encourage the opportunity for these new developments to be demonstrated. The MSG also plays the role of a buffer between the LEA and community groups, as well as between the LEA and potential bidders. It provides assistance to the LEA during the proposal evaluation and operational stages on an "as needed" basis.

As operational results during the initial stages are determined, the group provides program planning assistance to the LEA so that the instructional programs are effectively and efficiently "turnkeyed" into the school. In this way, the school can achieve the potential benefits which have been demonstrated. Too often, school systems either adopt programs not proven or acquire techniques proven in pilot programs only. Later they sometimes discover that the results erode over time. The MSG can provide critical technical assistance to the school officials during the adoption or turnkey process, ranging from projecting administrative costs required within the system to the implementation of performance budgeting techniques that will insure continuing quality assurance.

The *independent education accomplishment audit* (IEAA) is a managerial tool to assist quality control of the program. By reporting on results, this procedure encourages responsibility, creating a need for clearly stated performance objectives and an accounting for the costs incurred in achieving results. Just as the performance contract allows the school to monitor the contractor, the IEAA is designed to assure the lay board and the community it represents that the school leaders and the contractors are doing their work. The independent accomplishment audit, first introduced through ESEA Title VIII by the U. S. Office of Education, is a practical recognition that education is an important investment in human capital. Just as fiscal audits certify that public school resources and expenditures are (or are not) in balance, the IEAA certifies that investments in human beings are (or are not) successful according to stated goals and demonstrated accomplishment.

Patterns of funding the educational engineering process are critical. The flow of federal, state, and local funds must encourage the creation and responsible control of process components. Budgeting must be based on clearly defined criteria for "go" or "no go" decisions to be made at the end of each discrete stage. Three-stage funding as a facilitating device consists of resources and the timely freeing of previously earmarked funds for other new starts or operational programs.

The Texarkana Model

The Texarkana Dropout Prevention Program, under ESEA Title VIII, was first to use performance contracting with private enterprise in instruction. A number of new ventures have since been started, including those in Dallas, Texas, and Gary, Indiana, as well as the 18 centers funded by the Office of Economic Opportunity. These "second generation" approaches make use of performance contracts that are independently audited. They are built on the Texarkana approach and have employed techniques and strategies to overcome difficulties exposed during the first year of operation of the Texarkana experiment.

The assumption behind the Texarkana program and those of the second generation is that a private contractor will have greater freedom to innovate and thus be more successful in motivating students than the regular school system has been. A direct instructional service and a self-renewal function are the dual objectives of the projects.

Let me turn next to some of the wider implications of engineering accountability into public education.

Advantages of Performance Contracts

The advantages of performance contracts are inherent in the nature of the serious problems that confront education today.

First, contracting facilitates the targeting and evaluation of educational programs. Many good instructional programs have not been given the opportunity to demonstrate their potential due to the lack of an effective delivery system at the school level. Recent critical evaluations of Title I of ESEA note this operational inadequacy. The performance contract approach, which utilizes a separately managed and operated center with separate accounting procedures, fosters the objective evaluation of educational results and also the managerial processes by which these results were achieved.

Second, performance contracting for instructional services could introduce more resources and greater variability into the public school sector. Now, new programs are being offered to the public outside the school system; the process of fragmentation and competition has begun. Several large corporations are establishing franchised learning centers across the country. One company, for example, has at least 40 centers operating in the major cities of this country; 10 others are establishing centers in other cities. Performance-type contracts to improve student achievement in compensatory education are usually enacted between the parents and the franchisee. As a result, the parents pay for the schools' operations. As these franchised centers expand, parents may refuse to pay property taxes by defeating tax and bond issues. On the other hand, the performance contract approach would allow the school system to utilize the services and products of a particular firm or firms so that the public schools could be renewed through a turnkey process. Performance contracting can be looked upon as a means to foster and catalyze institutional reform within a school system, allowing systems to continue operations and to become competitive with private schools and franchised learning centers.

Third, the performance contract approach allows a school system to experiment in a responsible manner with low costs and low political and social risks. Both school officials and critics have expressed the need to determine the relative cost effectiveness of various instructional methods in contractor-operated centers, as well as upon incorporation into the particular schools. The performance contract approach not only allows for determination of these costs and benefits but also provides the bases for projecting initial adoption as well as operating costs when the system is introduced into the schools. In this way, the approach allows policy makers to make rational choices when choosing new techniques for extension into standard classroom practices.

Fourth, the new "bill of rights in education," proclaiming the right of every child to read at his grade level, will undoubtedly generate great pressures upon school resources. If our schools are to make this right a reality, they might want to consider using performance contracting for the development and validation of new reading programs. Upon successful demonstration, districts can then adopt the program or portions thereof. The success of these programs will in large measure depend upon the ability of the school to skillfully design and execute performance contracts and then effectively incorporate the projects into its normal operation.

Fifth, performance contracting can play a significant role in school desegregation. One of the major fears of the white community (rightly or wrongly) is that black children, upon integration, will hold back the progress of white children. Through the performance contract approach, many of the previously segregated black children will have their academic deficiencies, if any, removed on a guaranteed achievement basis while they are attending the newly integrated schools. From this point of view, performance contracting would allow communities to desegregate in a nondisruptive, educationally effective, and politically palatable manner.

Finally, the approach creates dynamic tension and responsibile institutional change within the public school system through competition. Leaders will now have alternatives to the traditional instructional methods when negotiating salary increases; performance contracting and its variant, performance budgeting, permit the authorities to couple part of a salary increase to increase in effectiveness.

Probable Trends

Whatever may be the merits of performance contracting, dramatic increases in its use are virtually certain in the immediate future.

Proper guidance, in the form of descriptive material as well as guidelines for implementing performance contracting and/or performance budgeting, is essential to avoid a potential backfire. For example, certain firms which develop tests and sell curricula might bid on performance contracts; other firms might develop specific reading and math curricula around specific tests. Franchised learning centers are bidding on performance contracts with schools in order to force state agencies to accredit their programs. Certain schools facing desegregation problems are considering very seriously the establishment of performance contract projects without a capability or an in-depth knowledge of the concept.

Two actions on the part of public policy officials would be helpful. First, additional operational proposals and planning grants should be funded, not only to legitimize the concept of performance contracting in education, but also to develop a "learning curve" on the "do's and don'ts" of developing RFP's for large urban schools. Because of the Texarkana project, those associated with its development have amassed a stockpile of knowledge; yet the applicability to diverse urban school systems is limited. Second, concurrently with the development of additional planning exercises and based on the experience of Texarkana, a booklet describing performance contracting and a procedures manual that could be made available to schools across the country should be written. The demand for such documents will increase dramatically over the next few months.

The Management
Support Group

The concept of the management support group is new to education. Its precedent was established in the defense-aerospace area when, in the mid-fifties, the Aerospace Corporation was created to act as a buffer and technical assistance team between the Air Force and weapons systems suppliers for the Air Force. The Aerospace Corporation's major functions were to develop programs, design requests for proposals based on performance specifications, assist in evaluating proposals, and provide management services to contractors. The major functions of the MSG in education under the concept of educational engineering would be in the following areas:

1. Program planning and development assistance School systems generally lack such a management capability, or, if such is available, "day to day" operations prevent effective utilization of that resource. Moreover, an outside group provides new insights and a different perspective in analyzing educational and other problems and in developing alternative solutions. For these and other reasons, it is advantageous for the school to have an MSG develop the RFP. The MSG could assist in the following ways during the program development and planning:

a. analyze and determine the community's educational needs and the desired levels of student performance;
b. conduct program definition phase studies and determine sources of funding;
c. develop the RFP and experimental design to be used for turnkey purposes as well as national dissemination;
d. develop and recommend "program change proposals" on a continuing basis during the initial stages;
e. develop means for gathering and maintaining political and community support for the program during all phases;
f. contact potential bidders in the education industry and R & D

(research and development) laboratories to insure that the latest innovative techniques are considered and are encouraged for application by the direction and flexibility allowed in the RFP;
g. determine the qualified bidders and send them the RFP.

2. Project management assistance. Too often, proposals are developed by outside groups who curtail relationships with the school once the contract has been awarded. The management support group has to provide extended and sustained services in the areas ranging from establishing the project management office to developing evaluation techniques. The project management services would be in the following areas:
a. develop a multi-year management plan for the conduct of the demonstration and turnkey effort, including an administrative system for the LEA's project management office;
b. conduct, when appropriate, pre-proposal development and bidders' conferences with all interested parties;
c. establish a proposal evaluation procedure and assist in the evaluation by presenting strengths and weaknesses to the LEA;
d. continually evaluate the contractor's progress and assist in contract renegotiations as required;
e. manage pilot programs when specifically requested to do so by the LEA;
f. analyze the administrative and managerial changes required when the techniques proven in pilot programs are integrated into the school systems. This turnkey phase is critical to overall success and requires careful analysis and program planning and budgeting.

3. Communications link. Because many firms of unknown or questionable reliability will be entering this newly created multibillion-dollar market, the MSG is a necessary mediator and "honest broker" between the firms and the school systems. At the community level, the vested interests of powerful groups and important decision makers must be determined. Here, the MSG, acting as a buffer between the LEA and these interest groups, both inside and outside the school system, can obtain such information in an effective and politically advantageous manner. (For example, the superintendent could point to the MSG as a scapegoat if specific ideas or recommendations are not accepted by the board.) The MSG can provide an on-call, as-needed manpower pool during planning and implementation. It can hire potential school employees in order to allow officials to see them in action. Moreover, the MSG has access to consultants around the country; on short notice

it can provide their services while bypassing cumbersome district procedures.

In short, the politics of experimentation where private industry, local schools, and the federal government are all involved creates the need for unofficial advocates and buffer mechanisms to protect politically all parties concerned, while insuring that the project does in fact become a reality.

Probable Trends

The concept of the management support group was made legitimate by the Title VII and Title VIII ESEA grant guidelines. Only a few firms have the capability to perform this function on their own, although many individuals do have this capability and could form a fertile cadre to advise and train others. The concept of catalytic buffers was included in the enabling legislation for ESEA Title III, presented to Congress in 1965-66; however, it was deleted in final legislation. Many people attribute the failures of Title III projects to the lack of a mechanism that would have provided the necessary political and technical skills to insure effective planning implementation and eventual adoption by LEA's of successful projects. A strategy for developing this capability within school systems across the country would reap enormous cost savings, reduce time wastage, and effect early adoption of new programs.

Independent Accomplishment Audit

Similar to the earlier demand for fiscal audits is the public's present demand for an accounting of student accomplishment. Just as the independent fiscal audit of schools has eliminated most fiscal illegality and has forced fiscal management changes, the IEAA group can also be used to create a demand for necessary instructional reforms. The concern for results in education among the electorate is a recent development, but it is gaining momentum. "Equal opportunity" in education no longer mollifies the majority: some "equity of results" is demanded. This is especially true of the educational benefits conventionally called the "basic skills." Even though Title I language reflects a traditional concern over inputs such as equipment, teachers, space, and books, the subsequent questions raised by Congress have moved beyond how the money was spent to whether the students have learned, have secured jobs, or are falling behind. This is the political soil from which the independent accomplishment audit has grown.

The independent education accomplishment audit is a process similar to that used in a fiscal audit. The emphasis, however, is on student performance as a result of financial outlays. The IEAA relies upon outside independent judgment and has six essential parts: the pre-audit, the translation of local goals into demonstrable data, the adoption or creation of instrumentation and methodology, the establishment of a review calendar, the assessment process, and the public report.

1) *The pre-audit:* The auditor selected by the school system starts the IEAA process by discussing with the staff, students, and community the objectives and plans of the particular program to be reviewed. This phase produces a list of local objectives and a clear description of the programs in some order of priority. In performance contracts, he reviews the project's "procedures" manual.

2) *The translation:* In concert with local people, the auditor determines what evidence will be used to indicate whether the objectives have been met and decides what methods will be used to gather the evidence. This phase produces a set of specifications indicating what the student will be able to do as a result of the educational experience, the manner in which the evidence will be secured, and the standards which will be applied in evaluating the success of the program in helping students to achieve the objectives.

3) *Instrumentation:* Along with the translation, the auditor, working with the LEA, determines the audit instruments, such as tests, questionnaires, interview protocols, and unobtrusive measures, which will be used to gather the evidence. The product of this activity is a set of defined techniques and procedures for data gathering.

4) *Review calendar:* An agreement is secured in writing which indicates the nature of the reviews, where they will be held, how long they will take, when they will occur, who is responsible for arrangements, the nature of the arrangements, and other logistical considerations. It is essential that the calendar be determined in advance and that all concerned be party to, and have the authority to honor, the agreement.

5) *The audit process:* This is a responsibility of the auditor. In this phase, the auditor carries out the procedures agreed upon in the pre-audit, translation, and instrumentation phases as codified in the review calendar.

6) *The public report:* The auditor files a report at a public meeting giving commendations and recommendations as they relate to the local objectives. The report is designed to indicate in specific terms both accomplishments and ways in which the program may be made more effective.

Advantages of the IEAA

The IEAA is a new technique designed to put local school personnel and the clients they serve in a problem-solving mode of thinking. It is built around a financial core, since money is a common denominator for the heterogeneous elements of input, but its focus is upon student attitudes, skills, and knowledge. From the IEAA, a whole range of useful byproducts is anticipated. First, it may lead to a knowledge of optimum relationships between outputs and inputs—for example, the "critical mass" in funding different types of compensatory programs. Second, it can form a basis for the discovery and improvement of good practice in education. Third, the IEAA creates the need for performance-type contracting and/or budgeting in the basic academic and vocational skill areas. Finally, it can renew credibility in the educational process by effecting more responsiveness to the needs of children and supplying the understanding necessary to produce change. The power of the electorate over public education must be politically, not administratively, derived. If techniques can be developed to convince the community of the benefits of responsible leadership through accountability for results, those interested in furthering education can better support the educational enterprise.

Probable Trends

The IEAA concept is now a reality. Over 20 groups or individual auditors across the country are receiving special training and guidance at USOE-sponsored audit institutes. Most of these groups will serve as auditors in Title VII and VIII of ESEA. However, if Title I and Title III funds were made available in a way that would allow LEA's to use performance contracting, and a large number (say 500) decided to do so, the existing resources for training and conducting professional educational audits would probably be inadequate. A superficial survey of existing USOE resources (Title

III service centers, the regional laboratories, and resources of private firms) indicates that the auditing capability is limited. A full-scale inquiry should be undertaken. At the same time, university-based graduate studies on educational engineering with heavy emphasis on educational audits should be instituted in a select number of qualified universities. Such curricula must be developed in light of the political and social milieu in which the audit must take place and must be conducted by qualified individuals who understand the concept from a theoretical as well as operational point of view.

Summary

The educational engineering process described above is consciously directed toward increasing the capability of the schools. Thus it is that a turnkey arrangement is called for in every RFP and is incorporated into every performance contract. With costs underwritten by the local education agency, provision for adaption, adoption, and installation of a successfully completed performance contract is assisted by using school personnel as consultants and as trainees in the process successfully bid by the contractor. The turnkey, or turnaround, feature is potentially a bodkin's point to pierce the armor of resistance to change and innovation that is so permanent a feature of school life. The objective of the standard turnkey feature of all performance contracts with private enterprise is simple and clear: to arm the school with the know-how of better instructional practice and to see that validated practice is adopted.

In general, educational organizations are influenced by three basic factors: the cultural or belief system, which sets policy in the form of goals and creates the mind-set by which activities are accepted; the technology, which determines the means available for reaching these goals; and the social structure of the organization in which the technology is embedded. An educational engineering process to produce accountability for results in the public schools attends constructively to these three basic factors.

V

Accountability in Education

John W. Porter

There are three aspects to the topic I am to discuss . . . But before talking about these three aspects, a general definition of accountability in public education seems in order:

Accountability is not performance contracting. Accountability is not program budgeting (PPBS). Accountability is not cost effectiveness. It is not testing nor is it merit pay for teachers, or a means of relieving teachers of their jobs.

Accountability is the guarantee that all students, without respect to race, income, or social class, will acquire the minimum school skills necessary to take full advantage of the choices that accrue upon successful completion of public schooling, or we in education will describe the reasons why.

What accountability probably means to the adult layman is returning in part to what existed in the 30's and 40's; a move away from the so-called permissive days of the 50's and 60's. But this time instead of the "produce, slide through, or fail" responsibility being on the student, the accountability emphasis is envisioned as a "produce or change" concept assigned as the responsibility of the educational establishment.

For a moment, let me share with you the beliefs that I have, and that I believe we should all have, in regard to public education, and why there is a need for educational accountability.

First, I believe that public education must guarantee that nearly all of the young people—those children in our elementary schools—will acquire competencies in the basic skills of reading, writing, and arithmetic, regardless of their socio-economic background. This does not mean any leveling off on the development of the whole child. It does mean altering the educational delivery system in whatever way is necessary to insure that the daughter of the unskilled ghetto worker gains from the kindergarten the educational choices that presently accrue to the son of a college professor.

Secondly, I believe that our public education, particularly in the secondary schools, must be programmed in such a way that the students will feel their secondary school experience is equipping them to be effective citizens in the adult society of the twenty-first century. We should be concerned when we see that perhaps two-thirds of all the work we do in our secondary schools is done to prepare 35 percent of our young people to go to college when, at the same time, nationally we have a third of our entering ninth graders failing to graduate.

For counseling effectiveness, we need to strongly consider the use of public relations persons on loan from business and industry to the secondary schools to supplement the professionally-oriented counselors. If the status of the world of work is to change to meet existing manpower needs, and if we are to demonstrate that everyone doesn't need to go to college to teach, we could well benefit from this "outside" contact for our pupils on a regular basis, not just the "career day" type of exposure.

We should also be concerned about the accountability of a system that seems to get the 6'5" basketball or football star through the academic mazes and to an attractive salary, while being ill-equipped to meet the needs of his 5'6" brother.

Third, I believe acceptable public education is going to require that we educators be responsible for seeking out, establishing and coordinating effective programs of adult continuing education which meet the needs of welfare mothers, the underemployed, the housewives, and the everyday workers that want some vocational skills.

When our educational system is so streamlined and so exceptional that it is able to respond to the needs of most of our 200 million citizens in regard to these goals, then and only then will we be carrying out our educational commitment to the citizens of our country and be achieving a degree of accountability.

Dr. Leon Lessinger, former Associate Commissioner for Elementary and Secondary Education in the U.S. Office of Education, stated: "Today the questions focus on results obtained for resources used. The questions are pointed, insistent and abrasive."

I for one welcome the questions and hopefully we as a profession will want to respond to them with alacrity.

The challenge is clear in my mind and I hope in yours. We must start to guarantee student performance, one aspect of accountability in the future; and you don't do this by instituting remedial programs to correct deficiencies in secondary schools. We must begin to guarantee year by year growth, starting in the elementary schools. Such an undertaking presupposes clearly spelled out performance objectives and criteria references for measurement. Criteria references for measuring student performance would presuppose an agreed upon level of competency in tasks that were being undertaken by the students.

Many of the principles underlying performance contracts and the more general concept of accountability when put together are worthy of consideration and utilization by all teachers. We will have accountability in the future. Accountability should be welcomed by the teaching profession, since the ultimate result is improved teacher performance and possible increased teacher salaries, not abdication of professional prerogatives.

Several aspects of accountability we can expect in the future which are currently being looked upon with skepticism are:

1) Paying for results rather than promises.
2) Designing performance objectives to evaluate the instructional procedures.
3) Identifying each student's characteristics and entrance level.
4) Specifying in advance desired outcomes of individual student performance.
5) Testing the instructional sequences to see if they achieve what they purport to achieve.
6) Reordering instructional strategies and personnel based upon student needs, abilities, interest and attitudes.
7) Involving the parents of the community in the educational process right in the classroom.
8) Informing students, parents and taxpaying citizens what we can and cannot do in a given situation and why.

These eight factors are difficult to refute. They answer the very basic question of "What if a student does not reach the objectives?" That is, we as educators have to be prepared in the future to tell students and their parents that the student hasn't achieved; he needs more summer work, or extended day or week help, or the diploma he will receive is for attendance, not achievement. Accountability of the future means not passing students from level to level because of chronological age and presence in the daily classroom.

The eight factors cited are difficult to incorporate into everyday classroom use given the way classrooms are now organized. But accountability in the final analysis is nothing more than better management by the teacher in the classroom, by the principal in his or her office, and by the superintendent at his conference table. For this simple reason, accountability will become almost a household word and acceptance is the future of accountability that is assured. . . .

Accountability, whether or not we want it, is going to be a part of the educational scene in the 70's. The important issue for teachers and administrators is that the failures of the past and present cannot be allowed to rest solely upon the shoulders of the educational community. If we accept this, then let us look at these three questions:

I. What educational improvement is it reasonable to expect for the future application of techniques of accountability? How will they be obtained?

II. What are the probable sources of resistance to accountability, and how can such resistance from within and from outside the educational institution be overcome?

III. What important defects in the educational system are likely to remain unaffected by accountability?

Let us now review some of the possible educational improvements which might come about as a result of using techniques of accountability.

I. Objectives of Accountability

Schools traditionally have not been problem-solving agencies. Schools traditionally have not focused upon cost effective management techniques in the classrooms. And most schools have not been held responsible for student performance.

Future improvements in education as a result of innovative techniques will be based in part upon the development of two specific types of information by local school districts.

1) Improved and more comprehensive student performance measures in the cognitive as well as affective domains, and

2) Improved and more specific performance objectives related to the functions and contributions of teachers, principals, administrators, school boards and the parents of students.

At present, such information does not to a great extent exist in school systems. As a result, a major consideration in moving toward accountability must be development of data gathering information systems and analytical assessment of the data gathered.

If properly managed, such an arrangement should result in a school system operation based upon some clearly spelled out objectives. Felix M. Lopez labeled this "management by objectives" in a recent article entitled "Accountability in Education."

This process requires a school district:
1) to identify the common goals at all grade levels for all subjects provided;
2) to think through its management procedures or delivery system in terms of pre-testing and post-testing as they relate to responsibilities of teachers;
3) to evaluate each student's performance in accordance with some overall efforts, or specify why such performance cannot be achieved. If we fail to evaluate, while we may know exactly what we are doing, we will never know what we have done;
4) to assure that school district goals are translated into performance objectives understood by students and parents alike;
5) to reach an understanding of steps to take when the child does not reach the minimum level of proficiency at the originally agreed upon specified time.

To amplify or clarify these points in terms of educational improvements which might be derived by the application of techniques of accountability, one needs to look at what our common goals are in terms of "grade level" performance. In essence, four educational improvements should emerge:
1) Improved teacher classroom management and professional performance;
2) Improved student academic achievement especially by the lower half of the classroom distribution;
3) Improved student attitudes and behavior;
4) Improved reporting of student progress in terms of student-school-community relations.

Further techniques of accountability should help remove the "blackboard curtain" created by the construction of classrooms on a 30 to 1 basis. Accountability to be effective will have to permeate through the closed-door classroom. Thus each teacher working with parents and others at each level will have to decide what exactly are the classroom expectations. In the fourth grade for example, we must ask, "What is it we want fourth graders to know when they have finished a year in our classroom?"

This concept of accountability focuses upon educational improvement by level and subject and as some have suggested could result in a marriage between technology and personal pedagogy, with the emphasis on measuring individual student progress.

Another dimension of the future of accountability for improving education must result in less student absenteeism, fewer dropouts, less special education, less fear of actually failing a grade, or less fear of "sliding through" feeling inadequate for the next level, lower teacher turnover, and less family mobility during the school year.

The improvements I have described will be obtained through local initiative resulting in a reordering of priorities, from successful performance contract arrangements, from new leadership directives, from state departments of education and from state and federal appropriation specifications.

Let us now talk about our second basic question—who will oppose accountability, and how can we overcome such opposition?

II. Resistance to Accountability

There are significant numbers of individuals in at least eight groups that may oppose the concept of accountability as I have defined it: 1) students, 2) teachers and principals, 3) central administrative staff, 4) school board members, 5) taxpayers, 6) legislators, 7) teacher training instructors, and 8) state department of education personnel.

Some students may resist the concept since it will focus on their performance in certain areas. Common educational objectives are desired; however, when these conflict with individual student preferences, an accommodation must be reached. Such accommodation, however, does not mean acquiescing, but spelling out in clear, precise language the alternative available.

Some teachers may not support the accountability concept because it implies that their work is being evaluated—and this is disconcerting to some individuals. In addition, some teachers' associations may oppose the concept on the basis that it implies an evaluation of the entire teaching profession.

Some central administrators, including middle management, may resist the concept of accountability—not because of a desire to avoid involvement, but because it may imply that outside assistance be brought in. This assistance may be a threat to the established practices of administrators. However, one of the major fallacies of educational management is that all, or nearly all, schools must be run in the same manner: they start at promptly 8:30 A.M. and close at exactly 3:30 P.M.; students are enclosed in units called "classrooms" except when they are allowed outside for recess or to pass between classes; all students are given the same curricula, and so on. The accountability concept may seriously challenge standardized practices—particularly in school systems where significant proportions of students have been shown to be failing.

It is likely that school board members will generally favor the accountability concept as it holds the promise of alleviating educational problems at little cost; however, if the concept is seen as one that requires additional monies, it is likely that many school boards will balk at the idea. Local taxpayers, too, will favor the idea—so long as it does not cost additional tax dollars.

State legislators are a mixed lot of ideologies and experiences, and they carry a variety of expectations for the schools. It is difficult to predict their feelings as a group—however, they will carefully scrutinize any concept that may cost additional monies, and one senses that they are currently not as appreciative of how well the public schools are working as they might be, in some situations with justification.

Teacher training institutions are frequently wary of innovations. It seems as if evaluations are conducted, but we too seldom see actual changes in practice. Why does this occur? Who, or what, stills the program? It is likely that increased accountability in the elementary and secondary school settings will result in increased pressure on the teacher trainers and their administrators to turn out more graduates who can guarantee performance.

Finally, some staff members of state departments of education will resist the concept because it will mean a drastic reordering of priorities and activities for them. The states are thought by many to be constitutionally responsible for education. If states are to take a leadership role in exercising this responsibility, it is likely that at least six implications will emerge.

1) State departments may be required to standardize educational assessment of pupil progress;
2) State departments may be required to develop uniform local budgetary procedures;
3) State departments may be required to establish procedures for equalizing financial resources by district;
4) State departments may be required to adopt guidelines for the reorganization of school districts;
5) State departments may be required to get involved in teacher negotiations;
6) State departments may be required to move from locally defined regulatory service and consultative subservient agencies to monitoring and management support agencies.

Chief State School Officers and State Boards of Education will have to assume a leadership role not only in establishing in-service training for their own staffs, but also for encouraging regional staffs within their states to tune in, as well as establish immediate discussions with the various professional groups directly affected by the concept.

In responding to the second part of this question, let me state, there is no panacea to overcome the resistance to accountability;

however, the complete involvement of those directly affected will help. Aaron Wildavsky, writing in the *Phi Delta Kappan* journal in December, 1970, is right when he states, "no plan for accountability can succeed unless all the major participants in the educational process . . . see something in it for themselves."

Many good teachers may, with the proper involvement in accountability, overcome the emotional trauma of having a class of failing students, if shown how such techniques can provide direction and support against arbitrary administrative decisions. At the same time, principals may begin to view accountability as an added leverage for dealing with the ineffective teacher. The other six groups of the eight, once involved and when we have identified clearly the specific benefits for them, may accept the pain of raising more money, for example, rather than opposing the concept. Different strategies and forces would be the deciding factors, based on the local and state conditions. In any event, communication in regard to the accountability concepts must be conveyed in such a way that all groups can accept the ultimate objective, improved educational performance, at a cost which can be justified.

We have talked about what accountability can do, and how to go about getting it, and we have talked about some of the difficulties of obtaining accountability.

Let's now look at what are some of our problems that accountability cannot overcome.

III. Limitations of Accountability

As mentioned, implementation of the accountability concept will not alleviate all of the problems of our educational system. A number of vexing socio-educational views will remain, including:

1) the issue of how monies should be allocated to schools in order to best facilitate equality of educational opportunity;

2) the issue of how educational monies should be collected in order to best facilitate an adequate and fair source of school support;

3) the issue of how teachers should be certified to teach in the schools in order to facilitate our best college students going into the professions with the best possible preparation;

4) the issue of constructing school facilities that will adequately and fairly serve the next generation of students;

5) the issue of how the often ponderous educational bureaucracy can best be organized so as to facilitate a new sense of urgency and of innovative leadership that will respond more adequately and quickly to societal needs; and

6) the complex issues surrounding student disinterest and disaffection which mirror a more pervasive societal crisis.

In summary, I have defined accountability of the future as a quality or state of education whereby educational institutions take responsibility for insuring that their students reach agreed-upon and clearly-defined educational objectives, or explain why not. I have further discussed two aspects of accountability: 1) possible benefits to the educational system that may result from widespread adoption of the concept, and 2) possible sources of resistance to accountability. As a third point, I have spoken briefly of the problems that face us—and will still face us even if we attempt to hold our schools "accountable."

Let me conclude by stating that I think the movement toward accountability in education can be a healthy one as it can help to insure that all children will be served by the schools. However, let me also close with a warning: accountability for the future is not a panacea; the major problems of this society and its schools will not be solved without a national, state and local re-ordering of priorities and without an equalization of the educational, social, and political opportunities available to our children, youth and adults.

Maybe the most beneficial outcome of the future in accountability will be a complete shift in the role of the school, which has up to now professed to be committed to meeting the needs of all the children of all of the people. The possible overstatement, sad to say, is one of the big reasons for the current controversy over public schools. Accountability, more than any other single concept, will in the future force all of us as educators to examine this all embracing goal or American ideal. We need to seriously ask ourselves, "Are there institutions other than the school that might be or could be used to assist some of the children of some of the people in accomplishing some of the tasks?"

The future of accountability, whether the emphasis remains on efforts to relate "educational inputs" to "student output", or whether the emphasis is on patron choice, that is vouchers, free schools, open enrollments or parochiaid, school officials will in the future have to face each issue by answering clearly six specific questions.

1. What are the common and specific goals to which the teacher and school is striving?
2. What student, community or societal needs inventories are available, on paper, to indicate change strategies which should be undertaken?
3. What specific and measurable performance objectives have

been written down that would enable parents, students and teachers to understand the minimum expectations of the unstructured programs?

4. What analysis of the existing delivery system is available to indicate that the current educational input approach is manageable and defensible as compared to alternatives?

5. What forms of testing and evaluation will be undertaken to enable the "at large community" to know whether or not the delivery system measured up to the performance predictions?

6. What recommendations are the school systems ready to make as a result of the testing and evaluation data?

Perhaps we have always had accountability—we always checked out what went into education—facilities, materials, attendance, hot lunches—but too inconsistently did we "do something" new about what came forth; what pupils learned; what skills were obtained. In fact, we went out of our way to find excuses for those children who did not learn—broken homes, language barriers, ethnic or national background, malnutrition. That is, we placed too much responsibility for success upon the student and his parents. But, if the student didn't perform, we began passing him up the educational ladder anyway. What is envisioned now is a strengthening of the role of the teacher, so that he or she is not placed in such a situation. The future, as accountability becomes firmly entrenched, will allow for very few excuses. We educators will be responsible for failure, and the exciting, fantastic goal before us is to have *achievement* realized by nearly the total school population, and I am convinced the educational community, . . . will respond to this challenge.

Bibliography

"Accountability: A Way to Measure the Job Done by Schools." *The New York Times.* Sunday, February 14, 1971.

"Accountability for Whom? for What?" Editorial *Phi Delta Kappan*, December, 1970, p 193.

Bain, Helen, "Self-Governance Must Come First, Then Accountability," *Phi Delta Kappan*, p 413.

Barro, Stephen M. "An Approach to Developing Accountability Measures for the Public Schools," *Phi Delta Kappan*, December, 1970, p 196-205.

Darland, D. D., "The Profession's Quest for Responsibility and Accountability," *Phi Delta Kappan*, September, 1970, p 41-44.

Davies, Don, "The Relevance of Accountability," *Journal of Teacher Education*, Spring, 1970, p 133.

————— , "They Said This: Abstracts of Recent Addresses," *The Journal of Teacher Education*, Spring, 1970, p 127-133.

Dolan, Patrick, "Performance Pacts Are Arriving," *Teacher's Voice* (Michigan Education Association) 8 February 1971, pp 1, 6.

Durstine, Richard M., "An Accountability Information System," *Phi Delta Kappan*, December, 1970, p 236-239.

Dyer, Henry S., "Toward Objective Criteria of Professional Accountability in the Schools of New York City," *Phi Delta Kappan*, December, 1970, p 206-211.

Elam, Stanley, "The Age of Accountability Dawns in Texarkana," *Phi Delta Kappan*, June 1970, p 509-514.

Lessinger, Leon, "Engineering Accountability for Results in Public Education," *Phi Delta Kappan*, December, 1970, p 217-225.

————, *Every Kid a Winner*, Simon and Schuster, 1970, New York: p 239.

————, "The Powerful Notion of Accountability in Education," *Journal of Secondary Education*, December, 1970, p 339-347.

Lieberman, Myron, "An Overview of Accountability," *Phi Delta Kappan*, December, 1970, p 194-195.

Lopez, Felix M., "Accountability in Education," *Phi Delta Kappan*, December, 1970, p 231.

Nottingham, Marvin A. and Zeyen, Louis D., "Commitment to Accountability—A Case Study," *Journal of Secondary Education*, January, 1971, p 3-8.

Phillips, Harry L., "Accountability and the Emerging Leadership Role of State Education Agencies," *Journal of Secondary Education*, December, 1970, p 377-380.

Silber, John R., "The First Hurrah," *Newsweek*, 4 January 1971, p 32.

Wildavsky, Aaron, "A Program of Accountability for Elementary Schools," *Phi Delta Kappan*, December, 1970, p 212-216.

VI

Some Uneasy Inquiries
into Accountability

Dennis D. Gooler

In a recent study by Gallup the author makes a strong case for recognition of the changing mood of the public toward education:

People continue to have a high regard for the schools of their community and they believe firmly that education is the royal road to success in America. Yet there is undeniably a new mood in the nation with which educators must reckon.

Up to this point in history, the majority of citizens have been quite willing to take the word of the school board and of the teachers and administrators that the schools are doing a good job. They have looked with pride on the community's school buildings and its winning football or basketball teams. These have been good enough to convince many that the local schools are good. But evidence in the present study indicates that this way of judging the quality of education may be in for a change.(1)

Adults included in Gallup's study were asked: Would you favor or oppose a system that would hold teachers and administrators more accountable for the progress of students? The study reports that 67 percent of the adults voted in favor, 21 percent opposed the idea, and the remaining 12 percent had no opinion.

But what shape shall this accountability take? Robinson asks, "Accountability for whom? For what?"(2) And Lennon echoes the spirit of that inquiry: What are the schools to be accountable for" Who shall be accountable? How shall accountability be established? By whom shall accountability be determined?(3)

There are many definitions or descriptions of accountability in the literature, yet most definitions are strangely ambivalent. The dictionary definition uses words such as "answerable," or "explainable." One response to the question, "What is accountability?" was developed at the Center for Instructional Research and Curriculum Evaluation (CIRCE), University of Illinois. The response, contained in an introduction to *The Accountability Notebook,* is reproduced in full below:

Accountability is doing what is supposed to be done.

Accountability is often unknown because it is difficult to find out what is being done and because different people have different ideas as to what is *supposed to be* done.

Full accountability depends on people agreeing about what the goals are and on people knowing the progress toward these goals. Full accountability is impossible, but a high level of accountability can be attained.

An Illinois school that is accountable is one that is doing what it is supposed to do. It needs to keep teachers, students, parents, and other citizens advised as to what it is doing. It needs to continue to resolve—to find the best compromises for—the different needs and expectations these people have.

Accountability involves an assessment or estimation of what is, a judgment of effectiveness and/or worth of what is, and some form of attribution of responsibility to someone or something. Accountability requires disclosure of information by school people to those who demand such disclosures. Accountability is different from *responsibility*. We may not be required to offer disclosure of all those things we are *responsible* for, yet we continue to be responsible for those things. This writing addresses the problems of disclosure.

In this discussion, some inquiries into the question of criteria and standards used in accountability will be made. In addition, an inquiry into how we perceive what *is* will be pursued. This is a way of asking about the nature of accountability. The intent is to probe, not prescribe; it is generally easier to criticize than create, of course: it is hoped these inquiries will be responsible ones.

On Criteria

Educational accountability is concerned with determining how *well* the school is doing what it does, *and* whether it is doing those things it should. There is a need for a clear delineation of goals and activities, together with a clarification of the reasons for selecting some goals and not others.

The areas in which schools may be held accountable, by various citizens or professional groups, may be determined in part by perceptions of what things these groups or individuals think are important. That is, people may try to determine not only how well the school is accomplishing its goals, but also whether or not the school seems to be giving high priority to those goals it *ought* to be giving high priority to.

By what criteria shall we judge the effectiveness of our schools? The most popular criteria for determining success are those criteria concerned with certain specified cognitive learner outcomes. In performance contracting, for example, success is determined (and rewarded) by assessing gain as indicated by scores on standardized tests in specific subject matter areas. The problems of measurement related to this kind of criterion are numerous— Lennon(4), Stake(5), Stake and Wardrop(6), Barro(7). Cognitive achievement gain, as indicated by changes in performance on specified tests, appears to many to be more amenable to measurement than any other criteria, such as the measurement of self-concept, or alienation or logical thinking.

The criterion of cognitive gains certainly cannot be dismissed as irrelevant. If we could adequately measure learner outcomes (particularly in terms of some kind of gain) would we have captured the essence of what schools are all about? Would we have identified *the* criterion upon which the school should be held accountable? Not entirely, particularly if we place any credence in such data as that provided by Gallup(8) who indicates that any thought about the curriculum (meaning, presumably, learner outcomes, methodologies, content, etc) is relegated to only the seventh most important school problem, as viewed by a variety of kinds of people. Many regard so-called "non-cognitive" attributes such as love, sensitivity, or feeling as important goals for the school. Should these goals be reflected in judgmental criteria, and in our attempts to be answerable?

Few people would reject the notion that the school should be accountable for more than cognitive outcomes. Despite a general feeling that the school exists to do more than just promote certain specified cognitive outcomes, however, we may find ourselves judging the school only on that basis, because the cognitive outcomes criteria may be the only criteria about which we have tried to collect empirical data. In the absence of data on success in achieving other school goals, we may, for accountability purposes, consider *only* the cognitive outcomes criteria.

What are some alternative (or additional) criteria by which the school might be judged and held accountable? The call for change proposed by Holt, Goodman, Illich, Silberman, and others is, in part, a call for different criteria of judgment. Further indications of the need for change are reflected in much of the "student unrest."

Students are telling us we are not using the right criteria to judge their worth. They would hold us accountable for our failure to establish some goals they think are important, and for our inability to reach still others.

A number of people are beginning to think about the various needs in which the school has some responsibility. One example of attempts to conceptualize the broad nature of accountability is found in the CIRCE *Accountability Notebook*. The *Notebook* is intended as an aid to school personnel, to remind them of the various areas in which they might be required to disclose information about what they are doing. Figure 1 outlines four broad areas of responsibility and potential accountability (school audit, student performance, teacher performance, and administration performance), and lists within each broad area, certain specific areas.

FIGURE 1: FOUR BROAD AREAS OF SCHOOL RESPONSIBILITY

(From the CIRCE Accountability Notebook)

AREAS OF RESPONSIBILITY CONCERNING:

The School
    Fiscal
    Legal
    Moral

Student Performance
    Cognitive
    Affective
    Psychomotor

Teacher Performance
    Curricular content
    Teaching
    Support facilities and resources

Administration
    Routine operations
    Decision making and communication
    The school as a social institution

Part of the importance of this work lies in the expansion of ideas as to what should be the range of accountability criteria. The school cannot and should not be judged on the basis of one or two criteria alone. In reality, it is likely that different kinds of people will use different criteria for holding the school accountable. The CIRCE effort set forth a collection of possible criteria. There are undoubtedly others. The substance of the *Notebook* will have to be supplemented with many other perceptions of accountability, and, perhaps more importantly, it will have to be continuously updated as new issues emerge. The authors must have had this in mind when they determined to use a three ring notebook. Tomorrow may bring new and different criteria.

Some readers may regard all of this as a plea to return to no accountability, for certainly we are not very good at measuring many of the alternative criteria suggested in *Accountability Notebook,* nor are we particularly good at defining the *rationale* for why we should measure certain things. It is likely that we may have to set priorities; we may not be able to attend to all things. Deterline argues:

Education requires some form of commitment to a set of criteria. Unless we are willing to commit ourselves to a specific set of criteria, no "complete and objective evidence" can be obtained indicating that our students have or have not attained them! If we don't care about all of our students attaining at least some uniform minimum level of competence, then we can do without criteria, and quality control and accountability. We can then continue to present information and grade on a curve and let it go at that. Once we commit ourselves, however, and agree on a set of criteria—even if it is necessary to establish a tentative set of criteria, planning to improve that set as we collect relevant data— we can make accountability a viable concept and methodology. Obviously, I am referring here to the use of instructional objectives.(9)

Possibly true. The potential danger, however, is that agreement will be agreement among a selected few, and that those things agreed upon as criteria will be those presumably most easily measurable learner outcomes.

Judgment of worth, and subsequently accountability, is inexorably linked to goals and priorities. If we are at the moment very concerned about discipline in the schools, we will be little satisfied with data and explanation about student gains in spelling *until we have learned about the discipline problems.* At the same time, however, we may also hold the school accountable for maintaining a certain level of student spelling abilities. This suggests that accountability is a dynamic phenomenon. The predominant or important-for-today criteria for judgment change as goals and priorities change. If we honor in fact, as well as in rhetoric, the goodness of plurality, the desirability of multiple goals, we must necessarily consider plural criteria; there is also likely to be a number of criteria that appear in response to a given situation, and these criteria will constantly change as we succeed at some things, and fail at others.

In short, I have argued for the necessity of many criteria for accountability. We must begin to develop methods for telling how well we are doing in some areas, without losing sight of other relevant areas. But having a set of criteria is not the only problem. Accountability involves standards as well.

On Standards

Criteria represent variables about which people, looking at a program from various perspectives, might demand disclosure. Judgment involves not only the selection of variables, but the determination of benchmarks of excellence, or *standards*. Accountability requires the setting (implicitly or explicitly) of standards by which someone can define acceptability or excellence. Four salient characteristics of standards will be outlined below.

First, most standards are very difficult to explicate. Most of us have standards in very vague ways, standards which we find difficult to state, yet we feel them strongly. The extent to which we can explicate our personal standards depends in part on the issue being discussed. It is probably easier to state our standards concerning ice cream, than to state standards concerning desirable attitudes. Implicitly held standards do not seem to me to be any less legitimate or important than explicated standards: the point is that it is very difficult for a school official to deal with implicit standards, particularly when those standards are used as the basis for accountability demands.

Second, it appears that different people have different standards. What is excellent to one is poor to another. The significance of this characteristic of standards has been summarized by the well-worn phrase, "you can't please all the people all the time." The activities of the school involve so many people that accountability is necessarily very complex because of "non-standard" standards.

Third, standards change as do criteria. Standards are scales to be used with criteria. Standards seem to be closely related to expectations, as well as accomplishments. As we attain more goals, as we learn to do some things better, our expectations change, and so do our standards. We may not find our present telephone service very acceptable; thirty years ago our present service would have been regarded as phenomenal. And so in countless other situations. We have little documentation to suggest how much education standards have changed (indeed, even what they were or are) although we have a general feeling that standards are changing rapidly now. It can be expected that the demands for accountability will change as well.

Finally, I would speculate that standards are, for the most part, statements of a range of acceptability, as opposed to discrete points of good-not good. There are extremes: total rejection, and total acceptance—but most things are roughly categorized as acceptable or non-acceptable. Accountability, then, may be concerned with the school's ability to perform within a range of acceptability. The difficult part (for school officials) is trying to determine where the parameters lie.

The use of standards involves comparison. The comparison may be relative—the standard for one program may be another program. The comparison might be more absolute—the standard by which a program is judged may be a set of personal values held by the person judging. People make judgments using both kinds of comparisons. Just how these comparisons are actually made is somewhat uncertain; the process appears to be rather complex.

The point, of course, is that the use of standards is far from a simple undertaking. As standards are used in accountability, there may be a tendency to rely on few and simple standards of performance. Such a tendency should be resisted. We are again faced with multiples. Attempts to reduce the multiplicity to simplicity to continuously seek the lowest common denominator will necessarily lose something in the process.

Many would reasonably argue that our society must agree on some standards if we are ever to have a system of accountability. The potential difficulty is that we may get agreement on a level of specificity so general as to be of little help in making operational comparisons of output (or input) to standard. The situation *is* complex; we fool ourselves if we adopt some (arbitrary) standards for a few cognitive outcomes, and say we have solved the accountability problem.

The issue of standards has been stated elsewhere more eloquently than in this short treatment, but the intent of this brief look was twofold: to re-emphasize the notion of multiple perspectives of accountability (and thus to warn again of the dangers of oversimplification), and to forecast the probability of conflict arising because people will employ different standards in their assessment of what a school does.

On Getting It Together

There is a need to consider many criteria, and it is most likely that standards will change, and they will be different for different people. Those are powerful enough ideas, yet alone they would not seem to capture the spirit of accountability.

Fishell (personal communication) argues that the missing component is something called, for want of a better term at the time, "interaction accountability." That is, what are the operational implications of accountability when it is recognized that there exists some kind of interaction among the many criteria and standards that might be regarded as legitimate aspects of the examination of a school?

If attention is given to any one part of an educational program, less attention must necessarily be given to some other parts of that program. School resources are finite: it is impossible to attend 100% to more than one thing. Accountability requires the allocation or distribution of attention or concern among possible foci of concern. If you are demanding that the school be accountable and disclose information about X, you are of necessity requiring the school to invest less concern in Y, unless Y is a subset of X.

It appears that accountability is highly correlated with crisis. That is, if discipline appears to be of great concern to, let's say, a group of parents, because they see a lack of discipline, or they see it as a major problem (i.e., Gallup study), then that group will be likely to place the criterion of discipline very high on the list of accountability criteria. When discipline is no longer perceived to be a major problem, other criteria will be regarded as more important accountability criteria.

What is evident, however, is that discipline does not cease to be regarded as something the school is accountable for. Discipline will not be focused upon with concern *as long as discipline is not perceived to be a problem.* If the efforts and resources of the school, as well as the demands for accountability, are so directed to some other problem that discipline is neglected, then discipline will again become a problem, and will again become the focus of an active accountability. Here is where the notion of interaction, or displacement, seems important: there is some kind of relationship among the various elements of school operation, and notions of accountability must attend to these relationships. The school should not show evidence of accountability in one area to the exclusion of accountability in other areas as well.

It is possible that many of the school's activities and outputs may be regarded as routine, at least as perceived by observers. Activities are routine when they fall within some parameters of acceptability. The school is accountable for these routine activities and subsequent outcomes, but accountability in this case means not exceeding these parameters. As long as expectations are met, the public will not actively draw attention to those elements considered routine. Should expectations not be met, however, various publics may actively demand school accountability in the areas of those unmet expectations. The goal is often to "keep things running." The difference between running and not running is more discernable than the difference between running and running *well*. In addition, new problems may enter the scene, problems which present an individual with an unfamiliar situation, or with a situation about which he has no formal expectations or experience. These situations may become the subject of accountability demands.

The difficulty is that schools must, in developing an accountability plan, consider both those foundational (or basically static) areas of responsibility, as well as those situational (or dynamic) areas of responsibility. The weightings to be given to aspects of each remains a formidable economic, political, and educational problem.

It will not do to consider criteria or variables in isolation from one another. In our accountability efforts, we must be able to show what we gain (and what we lose) by establishing certain priorities. We must be able to show the pay-offs and trade-offs resulting from the patterns of emphasis we adopt. We must be able to document what happens to other disciplines, or attitudes, or skills development if the school decides to launch a major (resource-consuming) assault on reading deficiencies. Or what happens if the school opts for a more independent environment.

Accountability, then, must utilize more criteria for judging the school. Accountability must also take into account the intricate influences of action or attention in one area on other areas. To do so requires a much more comprehensive and complex view of criteria and standards. Given the inevitable levels of interactions, what kinds of criteria shall be employed? How can standards be determined? Difficult questions, to say the least.

But even if we could decide on what criteria should be used to judge the school, and if we could agree (or operate without agreement) as to what the benchmarks of excellence (or acceptability) should be, we have a third problem: What will be accepted as indicators of what is happening in a school?

On Indicators

Many of the decisions made in education are made on the basis of indicators, or some kind of behavior, idea, or phenomena thought acceptably representative of reality. Judgments of a program are usually made in response to an observation or description of something that seems to indicate what is happening in or as a result of a program. Some of us find comfort in saying that indicators often do not reflect reality, but it is difficult to know what reality *is*. Is performance on a standardized reading test indicative of a student's ability to read? Does a certain behavior indicate an attitude? The indicators relevant to accountability would seem to be dependent in part on the criteria being used to examine a program. That is, if the school is being held accountable for how well a student can read, some indicator of reading ability would be needed. For this criterion, skill in playing basketball might not be an appropriate indicator of reading ability. Parenthetically, it might be noted that the preoccupation with a certain indicator of performance (i.e., reading skill) may blind us to indicators of unintended outcomes. For example, in the process of learning how to read, the student develops a negative attitude toward reading, and thus reads only what he is required to read. Any notion of accountability ought to include accountability for unintended outcomes, negative and positive.

Indicators have some characteristics about which questions might be raised. Is a particular indicator an *appropriate* indicator of the state of something? A rather simplistic question, but one responsible for some debate. If I want to know if the school has accomplished goal X, is performance on standardized test Y an appropriate indicator? What is an appropriate indicator of an attitude held? Or a skill possessed? Or content mastered? Appropriateness, of course, is individually defined. We may need to seek agreement, or at least understanding, of what constitutes an acceptably appropriate indicator of the trait or behavior we wish to make some judgment about. Appropriateness is a particularly difficult concept when applied to indicators of the general well-being of an entire educational system.

How *sufficient* is an indicator? That is, does a given indicator adequately encompass the nature of what we are trying to look at? Too often, educators are prone to want to accept something very simple (or singular) as being indicative of something much more complex. The traditional example is the IQ. The danger is that the single indicator may shed light on only part of the behavior or idea being studied, and that that part may be regarded as the whole.

Edward Kelly and Robert Stake have pointed out a passage that was appropriate to some of their work, and seems appropriate here also.

A century ago the Swiss Historian Jacob Burckhardt foresaw that ours would be the age of "the great simplifiers," and that the essence of tyranny was the denial of complexity. He was right. This is the single greatest temptation of the time. It is the great corrupter, and must be resisted with purpose and with energy. (10)

Finally, how *observable* is the indicator? Are we presently capable of measuring or describing the indicator? Should we be trying to develop methods for measuring some indicators we can only vaguely see now? Here again is the recurring theme: Shall we restrict accountability because we do not now have the means of measuring or observing an indicator? Shall we say the school should be held accountable only for those things we think we are good at measuring? Or that we have time to measure? Or that we have the inclination to measure? Accountability may demand that we concern ourselves less with preciseness than with breadth, with approximating the whole of things. The call for new indicators is not restricted to education, but may be particularly *relevant* for education.

A plea for broader conceptualization of what accountability should be has been made. Questions, not answers, constitute the plea. What remains is to ask what will be done with accountability, where it will take us.

On the Uses
of Accountability

Accountability may reduce waste. Lessinger writes:

If educators can master the process outlined above—a process for engineering programs that work—overburdened educators will regain a spirit of excitement and mastery that has flagged in recent years. It can save society the long-term cost of allowing its schools to define millions of children as "failures."(11)

But it is possible that when "waste" goes, so may go the relevance of which Collins writes:

What do the accountability people think of those who desire to develop children's abilities to think independently. How do you measure, how do you "performance contract" for relevance, love, and independent thinking?(12)

Accountability may force us to examine our goals, and our methods of achieving those goals. But accountability may force us to pursue goals most easily attained, or most easily stated. Accountability may force a kind of naive simplicity on a complex phenomenon.

Accountability may demand the best from all of us. We may need to clarify, to experiment, to work harder to make things work. Teachers and administrators may need to be more sensitive to the broader community of which they are a part. And the community may need to become less passive, less willing to take the general word of the educator that all is well.

Accountability may take the best from us. It may ask us to refrain from the creative, the spontaneous, the unexpected. We may need to become more mechanistic, more specific-goal oriented. The educator may find his direction provided by others, not by himself.

Accountability enables us to show our merit. We can do our job, and assume our responsibility, because we know what it is. We can defend and justify our existence on the basis of our ability to enable learners to learn.

Accountability may make us up tight. Responsibility for gain and responsibility for failure is upon us, even though we may not be able, as individuals, to control many of the variables contingent upon student learning. We may be susceptible to political pressure; if we are different, if we espouse different values, we may be removed through some kind of misuse of accountability.

Accountability may enable us to show what we do with our dollars.

Accountability may force us to use our dollars in ways that we do not deem desirable.

Accountability may, for the first time, let us really see what we are doing.

Accountability may deceive us by making us think we are doing what we are not.

Accountability may force us to refine our techniques for measuring and judging what we do.

Accountability may force us to depend only on those things we can now measure.

Accountability may work for us.

We may work for accountability.

These are extremes, of course. How and for what accountability will be used remains to be seen, although it is likely that actual use will be characterized by a combination of some of the above.

Some have said that educators have never been held accountable for what they do or do not do, as lawyers or doctors reportedly have. But how do we determine when anyone or anything is being held accountable? Hasn't the student unrest on college and high school campuses demonstrated a demand for accountability? Aren't the schools told something when parents demand control over local schools? Haven't accreditation agencies fostered an accountability over the years? And don't I signal an awareness of accountability when I ask my daughter whether she enjoyed school today?

Isn't it possible that the school does reflect societal expectations, and is thus accountable? Isn't is possible that all of us have some undefined but real boundaries that tell us what the proper domain of the school includes, and don't we react when we feel those boundaries have been exceeded? Isn't *that* accountability? When we are silent, or only a little discontent, haven't we in fact said to the school, "We've judged your performance, and it falls within our range of tolerance." Have the schools ever *not* been accountable?

Accountability is deeply rooted in economics and politics. It addresses itself to the phenomenon of alienation, to the sense of lack of control of the citizen over the institutions that govern his life and his conduct. In times of tight money, accountability will flourish. And the politics of education shall not go unaffected by the move to formal accountability. One wonders if the *education* of the young man or woman, the boys and girls, will finally be related to accountability at all. And one wonders what criteria, standards, and indicators we will employ to determine the worth and the outcomes of accountability itself. What will we have gained, and what lost?

Notes

1. George Gallup, "The Public's Attitude Toward the Public Schools." *Phi Delta Kappan* 52 (1970): 100.
2. Donald Robinson, "Editorial: Accountability for Whom? for What?" *Phi Delta Kappan* 52 (1970): 193.
3. Roger Lennon, "Accountability and Performance Contracting," Paper read at the AERA Annual Meeting, New York, 1971.
4. Lennon, *op. cit.*
5. Robert Stake, "Measuring What Learners Learn." (Urbana: Center for Instructional Research and Curriculum Evaluation, 1971): mimeographed.
6. Robert Stake, and James Wardrop, "Gain Score Errors in Performance Contracting." (Urbana: CIRCE, 1971): mimeographed.
7. Stephen Barro, "An Approach to Developing Accountability Measures for the Public Schools," *Phi Delta Kappan* 52 (1970): 196-205.
8. Gallup, *op. cit.*
9. William Deterline, "Applied Accountability," *Educational Technology* 11 (1971): 15-20.
10. Daniel Moynihan, Remarks made to the Cabinet and Sub-Cabinet, East Room, The White House, December 21, 1970. (Press release.)
11. Leon Lessinger, *Every Kid a Winner: Accountability in Education* (New York: Simon and Schuster, 1970).
12. Donald Collins, "Accountability of Relevance," *American Teacher* 55 (1970): 12.

VII

Accountability: Possible Effects on Instructional Programs

Albert Shanker

I think the first thing that needs to be said about accountability from the point of view of the teacher is that the concept is very much feared. It is feared because accountability in its recent thrust to prominence has had at least three separate meanings.

The first meaning is associated with the schools where the parents say, "You, the teachers, are paid to teach. Our children have been going to school year after year and they are falling further and further behind. We demand that you be accountable to us. If the children don't learn we demand the right to remove you." So, in the first sense, accountability views the teacher as a hired hand, or a hired mind—or both—of a group of parents. Thus, accountability essentially means the right of that group to pick and choose, to retain or get rid of those whom it wants to; whether on the basis of adequate or inadequate information, knowledge, or judgment.

The second meaning derives from the great desire to control educational expenditures. How is the school accounting for the dollars that we are spending for education? How do we know we are getting our money's worth?

The third meaning of accountability deals with the development of professional standards. For example, there is a body of agreement in other fields, such as medicine and law, as to what constitutes competence and incompetence.

The fears of teachers, then, are dependent upon which of these three meanings is used in a given accountability effort, and the manner in which the objective associated with that meaning is achieved.

Teachers are also deeply concerned about the concept of innovation, which is so frequently associated with accountability. They have learned through years of experience—and rather bitter experience—that educational innovation in the American public schools has nothing to do with the improvement of education.

It is, instead, a kind of public relations device whereby the reigning political power—whether it's a school board, or the principal or school superintendent trying to convince the community that he or she is a bright, shiny individual doing all sorts of new and creative things—brings out all kinds of ideas which force teachers and children and others to march in different directions. A year later, that lot is dropped as a new set of innovations is produced like rabbits from a hat. These innovations, rather than being honest attempts at educational improvement, are really public relations efforts.

Further, there is a great discrepancy between, on the one hand, the educational change and innovation expected by the educational establishment and the New Left critics, and, on the other hand, what is actually expected from teachers in the classroom, namely, that the teachers are expected to maintain a rather high degree of order in a rather unusual situation. That is, you place 30 youngsters in their seats at 8:30 A·M·, and the teacher's prime responsibility is to keep them relatively quiet, relatively immobile for a long period of time.

Research has shown that this expected degree of order is based on a series of sanctions which the teacher has developed. And the students, in turn, have developed understandings with the teacher. They know, for example, that if they are not too disruptive, if they whisper quietly, the teacher will agree to ignore them, to withhold the sanction. Such a relationship can only be maintained if there is a relative amount of stability and continuity in what goes on in the classroom.

Unfortunately, change and innovation upset these understandings, with an ensuing risk of chaos and disruption in the school. We must remember that when an observer—be he parent, principal, or school board member—walks through the school, he rarely notices the wonderful innovations. But he's sure to notice how many kids are yelling and running around! It will not then be a satisfactory answer to say, "I was trying to innovate today, but it didn't work out. The kids didn't quite understand."

So, the teacher risks something with innovation. He risks those very understandings and relationships which tend to maintain the orderliness and quietness that parents seem to want.

Teachers are also disturbed by the frequent association of accountability with something called "teacher motivation," a doctrine which holds that many teachers fail to reach the children because they don't really want to. These teachers are accused of just being job holders—not really trying and not really wanting to do anything productive. Hence the calls for an individual system of punishments and rewards, geared to the children's progress.

This view of accountability poses a great threat, because, to be honest, most teachers *aren't* doing the best they can. And for a very simple reason: they don't know any other way of doing things. They are the victims, if you like, of a system that has seen eight thousand new teachers move into New York, for example, every year for the past twenty years. These new teachers, drawn from many different colleges and universities, are a remarkably diverse group: Catholics and Protestants, Jews and nonbelievers, blacks and whites, liberals and conservatives. Yet, after four weeks of teaching in New York City it is almost impossible to distinguish the newcomers from those they replaced. Which leads to a rather obvious conclusion: With the exception of the few outstanding figures who somehow operate on an individual basis, the overwhelming majority of teachers do what the school as a system compels them to do.

In these circumstances, it obviously makes little sense to talk in terms of individual rewards and punishments when the individual has no freedom to change his ways. It is exactly for this reason that [some] writers . . . are rejected by teachers. They are rejected because of the arrogance of the writing. Essentially, these New Left critics are behaving like a star of the Metropolitan Opera who criticizes his audience for being unable to sing as well as he does. Many of these books are written by self-proclaimed star performers for no other purpose than to say, "Look at all those lowly characters out there who are not as artistic as I am!" That, of course, is not very helpful to the ordinary practitioner.

Another difficulty with accountability lies in our present failure to use such knowledge as we already possess in a few vital areas. I will cite just two examples. The first concerns the findings of Benjamin Bloom, and others, that a major part of intellectual development occurs between the ages of two and five. Despite almost universal agreement on this point, there is practically no movement on the part of government—federal, state, or local—to develop an education program at that level. The second example concerns junior high schools. We've had junior high schools for about fifty years, yet it is tragic to reflect that, even today, 99 percent of the students who enter junior high school without knowing how to read, write, or count, leave in the same plight. School, for one of these youngsters, represents a context of failure, and in consequence, he does one of two things: He either drops out internally by just sitting in the back of the room, and will leave you alone if you leave him alone; or, he lashes out and becomes the violent and disruptive youngster that we see every day. This we know only too well, but over all these years nothing has been done to create an alternative model of education for such youngsters to identify with. We know, but we do not act.

With all these problems arrayed against it, how does one get teachers to accept this odd notion of accountability? To begin with, the first two conceptions of accountability that I mentioned must be firmly opposed. I think it is quite clear that teachers are going to reject the notion that they are just hired hands. Secondly, they are not overly concerned with arguments about budgets. Teachers will react negatively to statements that they must change their ways either because few or many dollars are being spent.

The third concept of accountability as being the development, with other groups, of common objectives is, I believe, acceptable to teachers, because strictly speaking it is not for teachers alone to determine what the objectives of education are. Nor are teachers as intractable on the subject as might be supposed, for they have already moved in this direction. In June, 1969, the United Federation of Teachers in New York City became, I believe, the first organization in the country with a contract clause stating that the Federation and the Board of Education would work together to develop objective standards of professional accountability, in cooperation with parent groups, community boards, universities, and other interested parties. There have been a number of meetings to this end, and, believe it or not, these groups which had been on opposite sides of the barricade in 1968—and which are still not friendly with each other—these same groups reached unanimous agreement on what they wanted.

The proposal has two parts. The first follows a management-by-objectives approach, with teachers, parents, students, community boards, the Board of Education, and supervisors at all levels developing agreed-upon objectives: objectives which are not so narrow as to turn children into machines, but also not so broad as to make measurement impossible.

The second part of the program is perhaps the largest research design ever put together. Its aim will be to identify the districts within the city, the schools, the programs, the materials—the individual, even—that are doing something to reach the objectives.

And, more important perhaps, it will also try to identify the factors which have nothing to do with the objectives, which are neutral; and those which are dysfunctional. This part of the program will include social, family, economic, and educational information in a form unlike anything seen hitherto.

The ambitious, far-reaching nature of this proposal suggests an important principle that is, perhaps, not too well understood as yet. But we must all come to understand it, eventually, if we are to make any progress with accountability. Simply stated, the principle is this: Where accountability is concerned, no man is an island.

Teachers do not work in a vacuum, a controlled environment with all random factors controlled. So it is impossible to develop a design that will tell you what the teacher should be doing, or which practices are good and which bad, without considering those random factors, or outside influences, that limit the performance of even the best of teachers. The individual student, his family, his socio-economic background, and the school system itself, must all be held accountable in degrees yet to be determined for everyone involved.

When this principle is clearly understood and freely accepted it will be easier for teachers to believe that a system of professional accountability does not, necessarily, imply an individual threat. For the inevitable effect of such a system will be changes in the structure of the school and of the school system in which it operates: Changes that will break the vicious circle in which each year, for twenty years, those eight thousand new teachers have found themselves. Changes that will bring about *change*. Simultaneously, large numbers of teachers will be persuaded to behave differently, because different demands will be placed on them.

Another by-product of a comprehensive system of accountability that is attractive to teachers will be a greater sharing of ideas. Very little has been done at the teacher level to create a bank of successful techniques. It's not being denied, of course, that we have grandiose schemes, master-of-arts degrees in teaching, and lengthy courses. But these are all a bit removed from the firing line, and, in consequence, we never hear of—or from—the teacher out there, somewhere: the teacher who, ordinary enough most of the time, proves to be absolutely brilliant for just three lessons a year, three lessons in which she develops certain concepts better than anyone else. I'd like to hear from her, and so would most other teachers. To develop better systems than we now have, we must pull together what is known out there—and use it.

This suggests, of course, that an essential part of any system of professional accountability is the development of a model of what constitutes competent practice. Competent practice is *not* necessariiy related to some particular performance result. It would be unwise to evaluate a doctor, for example, on the basis of the number of patients who die while in his care. If the doctor concerned is a cancer specialist, the difficulty is obvious. Here the question of competent practice may have more to do with whether he prolonged life for a time, or relieved pain.

So what is missing in our field of education, and must be developed in conjunction with the accountability movement, is a model of what a competent practitioner does when faced with a particular set of problems.

Speaking of problems brings to mind some that exist with three currently popular ideas. These ideas—vouchers, performance contracting, and school decentralization—all seem to possess either basic flaws in the reasoning that promotes them, or in the manner in which they are being promoted. Hitherto, I have been talking about accountability mainly in connection with its impact on, and concerns for, one segment of the educational community—teachers. But the three ideas that I've just mentioned should be of concern to all of us, because they can be serious obstacles to the development of a true accountability system.

First, vouchers—which are being proposed as a national answer to providing accountability by offering a choice to the consumer—the student or his parents. It might be more accurate to say "the semblance of choice," because no one seems to have considered the implications of a nationwide voucher system. So let us consider them, and to make things a little simpler we won't talk about the whole country, just New York City, much simpler.

Let's suppose that just 50 percent of the students decided they would go to private or parochial schools in the future. That's a small matter of 600,000 youngsters. Their decision would set off a chain of events, resembling nothing more than a child's game of "Ring Around the Rosie." With the public schools half-empty, half the teachers would be fired. Neighboring schools would be consolidated for efficiency and economy. Surplus buildings would be closed. The private institutions, besieged by 600,000 youngsters waving vouchers, would urgently need buildings, teachers, textbooks, and materials. And the only readily available source of buildings, of 30,000 needed teachers, would be those closed public schools and surplus teachers who are out looking for jobs. We have come full circle: The same children, in the same schools, with the same teachers. The great innovative voucher program has accomplished only one thing—it has removed responsibility from the government, because the schools are now private, not public.

Those who would drastically limit the scope of a voucher program in order to avoid these problems must necessarily turn the program into one available only to the elite few—a program hardly worthy of national debate and national support.

So much for vouchers. On performance contracting I want to start with the statement that, in a field as complex as education, there can be no guarantee of performance. The position is similar to that in other complex fields: a doctor or a lawyer cannot guarantee performance. If they did, they'd run the risk of being jailed as quacks. Perhaps those who purport to guarantee performance in education should also be jailed for quackery.

The second problem with performance contracting was foreshadowed by my call earlier for a model of what constitutes competent practice. Performance contracting moves us away from real accountability, away from analysis of what a competent practitioner should be doing, to consideration of a specific end product —away from the process which the competent practitioner engages in to the *product*, which depends on many factors not within the control of teachers or schools.

The next argument against performance contracting is that it seems to oversell an underdeveloped technology. I recommend to you a very fine book by Anthony Oettinger. *Run Computer Run* is a thorough analysis of the state of educational technology today. Like Dr. Oettinger, I am hopeful that eventually we shall acquire very sophisticated technology. I am not against technology, we need it, and we should develop it. But I am opposed to the manner in which the technology of performance contracting is being promoted. Performance contractors are behaving and talking as if a technological answer to all problems is already available. It isn't, and these companies should admit that they are trying to develop such a technology and need the children in today's schools to do it, that it is only a try, and not a cure for today's ills. Anything less than such frankness smacks of deception.

My fourth objection concerns the special motivational devices featured in most performance contracting programs. Radios, baseball bats, and green stamps are among the goodies being used. I'm not all that "holier than thou" about such things. I tell my son that if his report improves, he can have a new bike. We all use this approach, and there's no question that such rewards play an important role in our family life and our society. So we can't say that rewards must never be used, but we must ask some serious questions—because no one else seems to be doing so.

What happens to the student after he leaves the motivated, reward-oriented climate of the performance contract classroom and returns to a regular class? Does he refuse to learn? Does he fail to learn? Does the use of motivation in one room—which is not available to teachers elsewhere—create learning in one place and destroy it in another? And what happens next year, when the motivational goodies are withdrawn? I don't know the answer to these questions, and I suspect that no one else does, either. And because we don't know the answers, it is incumbent upon anyone who uses this type of reward system to build an analysis of it into the research design for his program.

Finally on performance contracting, I suggest a case of false packaging. I've already touched on the impossibility of guaranteeing a specified result, or level of performance. We are, of course, confronted with suggestions that this can and will be done. But what we are actually presented with is a *non*-guarantee. That is, it's not the student's performance that *is* guaranteed, but the contractor's payment that is *not* guaranteed.

We have even been oversold on the idea that the contractor doesn't get paid if the student fails. That just isn't true in the overwhelming majority of contracts. In fact, the contractor receives a succession of payments: when he signs, when he moves the hardware in, again at the halfway point, leaving only a fairly limited amount which he does not get if the children fail to succeed. In addition, many contracts absolve the company from responsibility for youngsters who fail to show up for the program a certain number of times—usually fairly small. So it is that we have in the Bronx a program with a tremendous amount of absenteeism, and the company stands to collect on the very students for whom the program was designed.

So the company gets paid a good amount whether or not there are results; it gets paid for the truants and dropouts, and it can also profit from a well-known characteristic of the standardized tests so commonly used today. I refer, of course, to errors of measurement. The simple fact is that if you tested a group of students today and again one month hence—having given them a vacation—25 percent of that group would make, or appear to make, one whole year's progress in that short month of vacation. If you paid the company for that group and repeated the cycle, at the end of another month the company would again be eligible for payment on another 25 percent of the remaining students. Non-guaranteed payments begin to look more like a mirage, I think.

I won't spend any time on the third obstacle to accountability—school decentralization. You all know what is suggested, and I am more concerned with calling attention to what seems to lie behind these three proposals: abdication, or evasion, of responsibility—or should I say, accountability—by the U.S. Government.

In the last decade, we have seen parents, teachers, administrators, labor unions, and civil rights groups marching on Washington to demand more money for education. Last year, the President suffered two major defeats when his education vetoes were overridden. The pressures are obvious and insistent, and the Administration is seeking ways to silence these clamoring voices. So I think these three proposals represent a national strategy for reducing the accountability of the U.S. Government to our school systems, our parents, and our students. In each case, when the voices cry, "Our children are still not learning," as well they may, the Government will have a set of ready-made answers available. "You decided on the school; choose another if you don't like it." Or, "So get another performance contractor." And, of course, "It's *your* Board of Education; you elected them. Elect another lot." It is a strategy to reduce accountability by creating a phoney image of consumer choice.

In reality, it is a strategy designed to take a major American institution, which has led to a good deal of social mobility and equality of opportunity, and to throw it away on a series of political gimmicks. These gimmicks should be rejected, for unlike many educational experiments which can be tried and, if they fail, be rejected, these experiments which reduce the commitment of government to education and which move the schools from the public to the private sector are, like experiments with hard drugs, irreversible. Our public schools, with all their faults, are worth keeping, and their improvement will come not from gimmicks but from the same type of slow, painful, unrestricted, free, scientific inquiry that brought other areas of human concern into the modern world.

VIII

Accountability
in Education:
The Shift in Criteria

Ralph W. Tyler

The clientele of American schools has always expected them to perform certain services and has made formal or informal appraisals of the quality and adequacy of their performance. However, the demand for accountability today differs in two major respects from earlier practices. The first of these is the definition of the tasks expected of the schools, and the second is the widespread belief that the schools are not accomplishing the tasks that they are expected to perform.

In an earlier day, the opportunities for professional, social, political, and industrial leadership were limited, and the schools were expected to ration opportunities for advanced education to conform to the opportunities for high positions. At the same time, the demands for unskilled, semi-skilled, and domestic labor were large, and pupils having difficulties in school or not finding schooling to their tastes were easily absorbed into the labor force without great regret on their part or on the part of the public. Without evidence from systematic studies of individual learning potentials, the public easily accepted the view that most children had limited potential for education and that the school's main task was to identify those talented few and to shunt others into useful work. Thomas Jefferson's design for the ideal University of Virginia involved "casting onto the scrap heap" the vast majority of youth who were thought incapable of much learning. Since most public leaders of earlier generations held these beliefs, one of the

important criteria for judging the quality of a school was its effectiveness in sorting its pupils. "High standards," including strict
promotion practices from grade to grade, was one index of quality.
Associated with it was a graduation policy for the eighth grade and
for the high school which denied diplomas to those who did not do
superior work on the final examinations. When Leonard P. Ayres
sixty years ago made his famous study of non-promotion and attri-
tion in the American schools, he found less than half the children
of each age group at or above the grade level expected if they had
made regular progress through the schools. A university professor
was quoted with approval who said to his students, "Look to the
left of you, look to the right of you! One of you will not be with us
next year."

A school was also judged by the public to be a good school if
those who were granted high school diplomas were successful in
college or were regarded favorably by their employers. School
boards commonly received from their state universities reports on
the grades made in college by the graduates who enrolled in the
universities. This criterion also placed major emphasis on sorting,
not teaching, and on advising students not to enter college if their
records were not superior rather than encouraging them to seek
more education.

Since there was widespread belief in hereditary talent as the de-
terminer of school success, the school rarely was blamed for
inadequacies in the learning of the pupils. However, the public was
concerned that the teacher "know his subject," so that the talented
pupil could learn from him. Hence, a third criterion used in the
public's appraisal of the school was the knowledge the teacher appeared to have of the academic subjects he was supposed to teach.
This was assessed in two ways—by the teacher's record in college
and by the reports of students about his knowledgeability as he
explained his subject.

The earlier view of the school's tasks recognized the will, the
habits, and the attitudes of the pupils as factors influencing their
education in addition to their innate capacities. A willful child who
went his own way without respecting the authority of the school
lost his own educational opportunities as well as distracting other
children from their duties. Tardiness, sloth and untidiness were
habits that seriously undermined educational development. Attitudes of disrespect for teachers and for rules were often contagious.
For these reasons, a school was appraised by the public in terms of
its maintaining discipline, and developing attitudes of loyalty to
teachers and the school. Laxness in discipline was the most
common cause for the dismissal of teachers when I was a public
school pupil.

Today's discussion of accountability by the school's clientele emphasizes the criterion of learning rather than sorting. It seeks to hold the school accountable for educating all the children, not simply furnishing opportunities for the elite. Although it expects law and order in schools, there is no consensus in the community regarding the elements of responsibility and freedom to be expected of children and youth. No wonder that school people are confused and concerned about the respects in which they are accountable and can report meaningfully to the public regarding the quality and adequacy of their services.

However, these changes and the resulting confusion should not cause us to dismiss as wrong-headed or impossible the current demands for accountability. The school has assumed new and essential tasks, and it must learn how to perform them effectively. At the same time, the public must be kept informed of the efforts and progress being made. To hide our problems under the rug is only to invite skepticism or even distrust from the school's clientele. And this has already developed to a point that in many communities, particularly in the inner cities and in other areas where children from minority groups are heavily represented, the lay leaders believe that the schools are failing their mission. Such a widespread attitude is new. In the past, at times, particular schools were believed to have deteriorated, but the conditions were thought to be unusual and the replacement of a superintendent, principal, or teacher would remedy the observed weakness. Generally, throughout the country, the school's clientele were confident that the educational tasks were being well performed. Under these circumstances, continuing constructive cooperation between lay and professional leaders was maintained. The loss of confidence among significant sectors of the population must be overcome by the development of mutual understanding and, eventually, of mutual trust. The current emphasis on accountability can furnish the drive for this development.

Although it is essential for the public to be informed about the learning goals of the school, and the progress and problems in attaining them, the assessment of what students are learning requires tests designed for this purpose. Most of the tests currently available are not adequate. The standard achievement tests commonly in use are not constructed to measure what students have learned but are designed to furnish scores that will arrange the pupils in a line from the most proficient in a subject to those least proficient. The final test questions have been selected from a much larger initial number on the basis of tryouts; these are the questions which most sharply distinguished pupils in the tryouts who made high scores on the total test from those who made low scores. Test questions were eliminated if most pupils could answer them or if few pupils could answer them, since these did not give much discrimination.

As a result, a large part of the questions retained for the final form of a standard test are those that 40 to 60 percent of the children were able to answer. There are very few questions that represent the things being learned either by the slower learners or the more advanced ones. If a less advanced student is actually making progress in his learning, the typical standard test furnishes so few questions that represent what he has been learning that it will not afford a dependable measure for him. The same holds true for advanced learners.

This is not a weakness in the test in serving the purpose for which it was designed. The children who made lower scores had generally learned fewer things in this subject than those who made higher scores and could, therefore, be dependably identified as less proficient. Furthermore, a good standard test has been administered to one or more carefully selected samples, usually national, regional, or urban, of children in the grade for which the test was designed. The scores obtained from these samples provide norms for the test against which a child's score can be related.

These tests—called norm-referenced tests—thus provide dependable information about where the child stands in his total test performance in relating to the norm group. But when one seeks to find out whether a student who made a low score has learned certain things during the year, the test does not include enough questions covering the material on which he was working to furnish a dependable answer to this inquiry.

This leads to another problem encountered when one attempts to measure what a child learns in a school year or less. In the primary grades particularly, each child's learning is dependent on what he had already learned before the year began and what sequence he follows. For example, in reading—some children enter the first grade already able to read simple children's stories and newspaper paragraphs. Measures of what they learn during the first year should be based on samples of reading performance that go beyond this entry level.

At the other extreme, some children enter the first grade with a limited oral vocabulary and without having distinguished the shapes of letters or noted differences in their sounds. Measures of what such a child learns during the first year must take off from his entering performance and be based on the learning sequence used in his school to help him acquire the vocabulary and language skills that are involved in the later stages of reading instruction.

A standardized test, however, is designed to be used in schools throughout the nation despite the different learning sequences they have, and with children coming from a variety of backgrounds and at various stages of learning in the field covered by the test. For this reason, it cannot include enough questions appropriate to each child's stage of development or measure reliably what he has learned during a single school year.

Recognizing that norm-referenced tests cannot meet the demand for measuring what children are learning in the school, efforts are now underway to construct and utilize tests that are designed to sample specified knowledge, skills, and abilities and to report what the child knows and can do of these matters specified. These tests are called criterion-referenced tests. Although there are few of these tests presently available, if the demand for the schools to report what students have learned persists, test publishers will probably respond with a crash program of criterion-referenced test development. Such instruments would furnish information about the progress and problems of the school in providing the kind and quality of service that the public is now expecting. A constructive dialogue can then be maintained with the community regarding the educational objectives, the efforts the school is making to reach these objectives, the progress pupils are making in their learning, the difficulties being encountered and the steps being taken to overcome these difficulties. Ample information on these matters can make the dialogue a constructive one and can reassure parents and the general public about the integrity of the school in meeting its responsibilities.

Bibliography

A. Books

Adams, John W. and Kitchak, Karen H. *A Guide to Performance Contracting.* Wisconsin Dept. of Public Instruction, 1971.

Browder, Lesley H., Jr., ed. *Emerging Patterns of Administrative Accountability.* Berkeley, Calif.: McCutchan Publishing Corp., 1971.

Burt, Samuel H., and Lessinger, Leon M. *Volunteer Industry in Public Education.* Lexington, Mass.: Heath and Company, 1970.

Committee for Economic Development. *Education for the Urban Disadvantaged: from Preschool to Employment.* New York, 1971.

Lessinger, Leon M. "Accountability: Its Implications for the Teacher." In *The Teacher's Handbook,* edited by Dwight W. Allen and Eli Seifman, pp. 72-82. Glenview, Ill.: Scott, Foresman and Company, 1971.

_____. *Every Kid a Winner: Accountability in Education.* Palo Alto, Calif.: Science Research Associates, 1970.

Stucker, J.P., and Hall, G.R. *Appendix: A Critique of the Theory.* Rand Memoranda #699.2. May 1971. (Bulletin)

_____. *The Performance Contracting Concept in Education.* Rand Memoranda #699.1. May 1971. (Bulletin)

B. Periodicals

"Accountability for Whom? For What?" *Phi Delta Kappan* 52 (1970): 193.

"Accountability Method Makes Failure the Teacher's Fault." *College and University Business* 49 (1970): 45.

Allen, D. H., and Lessinger, Leon M. "Performance Proposals for Educational Funding: A New Approach to Federal Resource Allocation." *Phi Delta Kappan* 51 (1969): 136-37.

Allen, James E. "Education and the Renaissance of State Government." *School and Society* 97 (1969): 148-51.

American School Board Journal. "Performance Contracting: Why the Gary School Board Bought It." *American School Board Journal* 158 (1971): 19-21.

American School Board Journal. "Two Out of Three Boardmen Buy Performance Contracting." *American School Board Journal* 158 (1970): 35-36.

Bahr, Jerome, "Educational Auditing: Here to Stay." *School Management* 13 (1969): 53-54.

Bain, H. "Self-governance Must Come First, Then Accountability." *Phi Delta Kappan* 51 (1970): 413.
Bair, Medill. "Developing Accountability in Urban Schools: A Call for State Leadership." *Educational Technology* 11 (1971): 38-40.
Barb, B. "Why our Schools are Failing." *Parent's Magazine* 44 (1969): 53-55.
Barro, Stephen M. "An Approach to Developing Accountability Measures for the Public Schools." *Phi Delta Kappan* 52 (1970): 196-205.
Bevans, K. "Accountability Octopus Gains New Territory." *The Times* (London), *Educational Supplement* 2871:11, May 1970.
Bhaerman, Robert D. "Accountability: The Great Day of Judgment." *Educational Technology* 11 (1971): 62-63.
Blaschke, Charles L., Briggs, Peter, and Martin, Reed. "The Performance Contract—Turnkey Approach to Urban School System Reform." *Educational Technology* 10 (1970): 45-48.
_____ and Martin, Reed. "Contracting for Educational Reform." *Phi Delta Kappan* 52 (1971): 403-06.
Bratten, D. "Performance Contracting: How it Works in Texarkana." *School Management* 14 (1970): 8-10.
Briner, C. "Administrators and Accountability." *Theory Into Practice* 8 (1969): 203-06.
Buelke, J. "Educators and Accountability." *Michigan Education Journal* 44 (1967): 25-26.
Bumstead, Richard A. "Lessinger's Logic." *Educate* 4 (1971): 25-30.
_____. "Performance Contracting." *Educate* 3 (1970): 15-27.
_____. "Texarkana: The First Accounting." *Educate* 3 (1970): 24.
Business Week, "Customers Pass the Test—Or Else." *Education Digest* 36: 5-7; November, 1970.
Campbell, R. F., and Layton, D. H. "Growing Expectations for American Education." *Education Digest* 35 (1970): 1-4.
Cass, J. "Crisis of Confidence, and Beyond." *Saturday Review*, 19 September 1970, pp. 61-62.
_____. "Profit and Loss in Education: Texarkana and Gary, Indiana." *Saturday Review*, 15 August 1970, pp. 39-40.
"Clouds and Controversy over Texarkana." *Nation's Schools* 86 (1970): 85-86.
Cooney, Thomas J., Hatfield, Larry L., and Vruggink, Elmer. "The Forum: Some Pros and Cons of Performance Contracting in Mathematics." *The Mathematics Teacher*, October 1971.
Cunningham, L. L. "Our Accountability Problems." *Theory Into Practice* 8 (1969): 283-92.
Daniel, K. Fred. "Moving Toward Educational Accountability: Florida's Program." *Educational Technology* 11 (1971): 41-42.
Darland, D. D. "Profession's Quest for Responsibility and Accountability." *Phi Delta Kappan* 52 (1970): 41-44.
Davies, D. "Relevance of Accountability." *Journal of Teacher Education* 21 (1970): 127-33.
Deck, L. Linton, Jr. "Accountability and Organizational Properties of Schools." *Educational Technology* 11 (1971): 36-37.
Deterline, William A. "Applied Accountability." *Educational Technology* 11 (1971): 15-20.
"Demand for Accountability." *Saturday Review*, 20 December 1969, p. 64.
Dillon, R. H. "Fine Art of Abdicating Responsibility." *Library Journal* 92 (1967): 2885-87.
Donovan, Bernard E., and Swanker, Esther M. "Voucher Demonstration Project: Problems and Promise." *Phi Delta Kappan* 52 (1970): 255.
Drummond, T. D. "To Make a Difference in the Lives of Children." *National Elementary Principal* 49 (1970): 31-36.
Duncan, Merlin G. "An Assessment of Accountability: The State of the Art." *Educational Technology* 11 (1971): 27-30.
Durstine, Richard M. "An Accountability Information System." *Phi Delta Kappan* 52 (1970): 236-39.

Dyer, Henry S. "Toward Objective Criteria of Professional Accountability in the Schools of New York City." *Phi Delta Kappan* 52 (1970): 206-11.
Education Commission of the States. *Compact* 4: 4-27. Covering the First and Second General Session of the Annual Meeting—Topics include "Accountability through National Assessment."
Education Turnkey Systems. *The Performance Contracting in Education*, Champaign, Ill.: Research Press (P. O. Box 2459, Station A.), 1970.
Education Turnkey Systems, Inc., 1660 L Street, N.W., Washington, D.C. 20036. *Education Turnkey News.* (Each issue gives information on developments in performance contracting.)
Ehrle, R. A. "National Priorities and Performance Contracting." *Educational Technology* 10 (1970): 27-28.
———. "Performance Contracting for Human Services." *Personnel and Guidance Journal* 49 (1970): 119-22.
Filogamo, M. J. "New Angle on Accountability: Rapid Learning Centers." *Today's Education* 59 (1970): 53.
———. "Texarkana Battles 'Dropout Dilemma'." *Elementary English* 47 (1970): 305-08.
Fox, E. J., and Levenson, W. B. "In Defense of the Harmful Monopoly; Merits and Limitations of the Voucher Plan." *Phi Delta Kappan* 51 (1969): 131-35.
Gardner, James, and Howe, Harold. "What Are Americans Receiving in Return for their Heavy Investment in Education?" *American Education* 2 (1966): 24-26.
Garvue, Robert J. "Accountability: Comments and Questions." *Educational Technology*
Geller, E. "Accountability: Right to Read Program and Integration vs. Compensatory Education." *Library Journal* 95 (1970): 1881.
Gillis, James C. "Performance Contracting for Public Schools." *Educational Technology* 9 (1969): 17-20.
Grayboff, Marilyn N. "Tool for Building Accountability: The Performance Contract." *Journal of Secondary Education* 45 (1970): 355-68.
Grieder, C. "Educators Should Welcome Pressure for Accountability." *Nation's Schools* 85 (1970): 14.
Harlacher, Ervin L., and Roberts, Eleanor. "Accountability for Student Learning." *Junior College Journal* 41 (1971): 27-30.
Harmes, H. M. "Specifying Objectives for Performance Contracts." *Educational Technology* 11 (1971): 52-56.
Harris, D. "Responsibility is Relevant." *PTA Magazine* 64 (1970): 24-26.
Harrison, Charles H. "How to Respond to Public Demand for Accountability." *Nation's Schools* 86 (1970):32-34.
Hottleman, Girard D. "Performance Contracting Is a Hoax!" *Education Digest* (1971): 1-4.
"How Education Groups View Contracting." *Nation's Schools* 86 (1970): 86-87.
"Jencks Tuition Voucher Plan." *America* 122 (1970): 517.
Jencks, C. "Education Vouchers." *New Republic* 163 (1970): 19-21.
Jenkins, Jerry A. "Planning for Classroom Evaluation of Educational Programs." *Contemporary Education* 42 (1970): 25-27.
Johnson, W. Frank. "Performance Contracting with Existing Staff." *Educational Technology* 11 (1971): 59-61.
Jordan, Bennett. "Educational Accountability: A Crucial Question." *Junior College Journal* 41 (1971): 23-25.
Kaufman, Roger A. "Accountability, a System Approach and the Quantitative Improvement of Education—an Attempted Integration." *Educational Technology* 11 (1971): 21-26.
Kennedy, John D. "Planning for Accountability via Management by Objectives." *Journal of Secondary Education* 45 (1970): 348-54.
Kirk, Russell. "Free Choice: A Voucher Plan; Giving All Students the Choice of Attending Either a Public or a Private School." *National Review* 21 (1969): 598.

Kruger, S. W. "Program Auditor: New Breed on the Education Scene."
American Education 6 (1970): 36.
————. "Accountability and the Educational Program Auditor." *Planning
and Changing* 1 (1970): 110-14.
Krull, R. P., Jr. "Accountability." *Instructor* 79 (1970): 16.
Lessinger, Leon M. "A 'Zero-Reject' Program in a Comprehensive School
District." *Journal of Educational Administration* 7 (1969): 2.
————. "Accountability and Curriculum Reform." *Educational Technology*
10 (1970): 56-57.
————. "Accountability for Results." *American Education* 5: 2-4.
————. "Accountability in Education." *Education Change Through State
Leadership.* Publication of papers presented at three meetings of ESEA
Title III personnel from state departments of Education, New York State
Department of Education, Albany, New York, 1970.
————. "Accountability in Education." In *Resources for Urban Schools:
Better Use and Balance,* edited by Sterling M. McMervin. Committee for
Economic Development, Supplementary Paper Number 33, pp. 23-48.
(Also published by Heath Lexington Books in hardcover.)
————. "Accountability in Public Education." *Today's Education* 59 (1970):
52-53.
————. "After Texarkana, What?" *Nation's Schools* 84 (1969): 37-40.
————. "Engineering Accountability for Results in Public Education." *Phi
Delta Kappan* 52 (1970): 217-25.
————. "Focus on the Learner: Central Concern of Accountability in Educa-
tion." *Audiovisual Instructor* 15 (1970): 42-44.
————. "Four Key Ideas to Strengthen Public Education." *Journal of Sec-
ondary Education* 45 (1970): 147-51.
————. "How Educational Audits Measure Performance." *Nation's Schools*
85 (1970): 33-34.
————. "It's Time for Accountability in Education." *The Nation's Business,*
August 1971, pp. 54-57.
————. "Quality Assurance in Schools: The Nation's Most Business,"
MASCD Journal 15-34, Spring, 1970.
————. "Robbing Dr. Peter to 'Pay Paul': Accounting for Our Stewardship of
Public Education." *Educational Technology* 11 (1971): 11-14.
————. "The Powerful Notion of Accountability in Education." *Journal of
Secondary Education* 45 (1970): 339-47.
————. "Teachers in an Age of Accountability." *Instructor,* June/July, 1971.
pp. 19-20.
————. "The Principal and Accountability." *The National Elementary Prin-
cipal,* October 1971.
Levin, H. M. "Making Public Schools Competitive: The Free Market
Remedy." *Current* 100 (1968): 25-32.
Lieberman, Myron, "An Overview of Accountability." *Phi Delta Kappan* 52
(1970): 195-96.
————. and Rothwell, Sheldon. "The Teaching Profession: Whose Responsi-
bility?" *Teacher Education* 21 (1969): 5-8, 19-20.
Lopez, Felix M. "Accountability in Education." *Phi Delta Kappan* 52 (1970):
231-35.
"The Low Productivity of the 'Educational Industry'." *Fortune,* October
1958, pp. 135-36.
Martin, Reed. "Performance Contracting: Making It Legal." *Nation's Schools*
87 (1971): 62-64.
Matzukus, John E. "Accountability and the Reverent Dogood." *Today's
Education—NEA Journal* 60 (1971): 57.
Mayrhofer, Albert V. "Factor to Consider in Preparing Performance Con-
tracts for Instruction." *Educational Technology* 11 (1971): 48-51.
McComas, J. D. "Accountability: How Do We Measure Up." *Educational
Technology* 11 (1971): 31.
McConnell, T. R. "Accountability and Autonomy." *The Journal of Higher
Education,* June 1971.

Meade, E. J. "Accountability and Governance in Public Education." *Education Canada* 9 (1969): 48-51.

Mecklenburger, James A., and Wilson, John A. "The Performance Contract in Gary." *Phi Delta Kappan* 52 (1970): 406-10.

Millman, Jason. "Reporting Student Progress: A Case for A Criterion-Referenced Marking System." *Phi Delta Kappan* 52 (1970): 226-30.

Morton, J. "Contract Learning in Texarkana." *Educational Screen and AV Guide* 49 (1970): 12-13.

Murphy, Betty. "Performance Contracting: Where Teaching and Technology Meet." *Opportunity*, 1 (1971).

Nash, Robert J. "Commitment to Competency." *Phi Delta Kappan* 52 (1970): 240-43.

National School Public Relations Association. "Accountability: The New 'In' Word." *The Shape of Education for 1970-71* 12 (1970): 19-23.

"No Magic in Vouchers." *Nation*, 29 June 1970, p. 773.

Nordh, Deborah M. "Emphasis: Accountability and the Community College." *Junior College Journal* 41.

Packer, N. A. "Why Teachers Fail." *Journal of Teacher Education* 19 (1968): 331-37.

Pell, C., and Quie, A. H. "Two Congressmen Look at American Education." *Childhood Education* 46 (1969): 17-21.

"Performance Contracting as Catalyst for Reform." *Educational Technology* 9 (1969): 5-9.

Peterson, Russell W. *Accountability in Elementary and Secondary Education.* Washington, D. C.: National Committee for Support of the Public Schools (1424 Sixteenth St., N. W.), July 1970. p. 4.

Phillips, Harry L. "Accountability and the Emerging Leadership Role of State Education Agencies." *Journal of Secondary Education* 45 (1970): 377-80.

Phillips, R. E. "Whose Children Shall We Teach?" *Education Leadership* 27 (1970): 471-4.

Prattle, R. "Public School Movement: Phoenix or Dodo Bird?" *Education Digest* 35 (1969): 1-4.

Roueche, John E. "Accountability for Student Learning in the Community College." *Educational Technology* 11 (1971): 46-47.

"Satisfaction Guaranteed or Money Back." *Saturday Review*, 15 August 1970, pp. 54-55.

Scheid, P. N. "Charter of Accountability for Executives." *Harvard Business Review*. July-August 1965, pp. 88-98.

Schwartz, Ronald. "Accountability: Special Editorial Report." *Nation's Schools* 85 (1970): 31-32.

_____. "Performance Contracting: Industry's Reaction." *Nation's Schools* 86 (1970): 53-55.

Stake, Robert. "Testing Hazards in Performance Contracting." *Phi Delta Kappan,* June 1971.

Stocker, Joseph, and Wilson, Donald F. "Accountability and the Classroom Teacher." *Today's Education* 60 (1971): 41-56.

Straubel, James. "Accountability in Vocational-Technical Instruction." *Educational Technology* 11 (1971): 43-45.

Swartz, R. "Performance Contracts Catch On." *Nation's Schools* 86 (1970): 31-33.

"Total 'Performance' Package Dispute Still Unresolved." *Nation's Schools* 86 (1970): 32.

Tyler, Ralph W. "Testing for Accountability." *Nation's Schools* 86 (1970): 37-39.

Underwood, K. W. "Before You Decide to Be Accountable, Make Sure You Know for What." *American School Board Journal* 158 (1970): 32-33.

Voegel, George H. "A Suggested Schema for Faculty Commission Pay in Performance Contracting." *Educational Technology* 11 (1971): 57-59.

Weber, Robert E. "The Early Warning System and the Zero Failure School: Professional Response to Accountability." *Journal of Secondary Education* 45 (1970): 369-76.

Wildavsky, Aaron. "A Program of Accountability for Elementary Schools." *Phi Delta Kappan* 52 (1970): 212-16.
Yengo, Carmine A. "John Dewey and the Cult of Efficiency." *Harvard Educational Review*. Winter 1964, pp. 33-53.

Related Professional Books from

Charles A. Jones Publishing

Curriculum Improvement for Better Schools, Jack R. Frymier, Ohio State University, and Horace C. Hawn, University of Georgia, 1970.

Behind the Classroom Door, John I. Goodlad, University of California, Los Angeles, M. Frances Klein, Institute for Development of Educational Activities, Inc., and Associates, 1970.

Toward Improved Urban Education, Frank W. Lutz, editor, Pennsylvania State University, 1970.

The Impact of Negotiations in Public Education: The Evidence from the Schools, Charles R. Perry, University of Pennsylvania, and Wesley A. Wildman, University of Chicago, 1970.

Humanistic Foundations of Education, John Martin Rich, University of Texas, 1971.

Guiding Human Development: The Counselor and the Teacher in the Elementary School, June Grant Shane, Harold G. Shane, Robert L. Gibson, and Paul F. Munger, Indiana University, 1971.

Innovations in Education:Their Pros and Cons, Herbert I. Von Haden, Miami University, and Jean Marie King, Alachua County, Florida, Schools, 1971.

Early Childhood Education: Perspectives on Change, Evelyn Weber, Wheelock College, 1971.

Charles A. Jones Publishing Company
Village Green   698 High Street
Worthington, Ohio 43085